Chambers
French
Grammar

Chambers

CHAMBERS
An imprint of Chambers Harrap Publishers Ltd
7 Hopetoun Crescent, Edinburgh, EH7 4AY

Chambers Harrap is an Hachette UK company

This third edition published by Chambers Harrap Publishers Ltd 2009
First published as *Harrap's French Grammar* in 1987
Second edition published 2002

ISBN 978 0550 10503 5

10 9 8 7 6 5 4 3 2 1

Project Editors: Alex Hepworth, Kate Nicholson
With Helen Bleck

www.chambers.co.uk

Designed by Chambers Harrap Publishers Ltd, Edinburgh
Typeset in Rotis Serif and Meta Plus by Macmillan Publishing Solutions
Printed and bound in Spain by Graphy Cems

INTRODUCTION

This French grammar from Chambers has been written to meet the needs of all students of French, and is particularly useful for those taking school examinations. The essential rules of the French language have been set in terms that are as accessible as possible to all users. Where technical terms have been used, then full explanations of these terms have also been supplied. There is also a full glossary of grammatical terminology on pages 9-15. While literary aspects of the French language have not been ignored, the emphasis has been placed squarely on modern spoken French. This grammar, with its wealth of lively and typical illustrations of usage taken from the present-day language, is the ideal study tool for all levels – from the beginner who is starting to come to grips with the French language through to the advanced user who requires a comprehensive and readily accessible work of reference.

This new edition boasts a smart new two-colour design to make consultation even easier and more enjoyable.

Abbreviations used in the text:

fem	feminine
masc	masculine
plur	plural
sing	singular

CONTENTS

CONTENTS

Contents

1 GLOSSARY OF GRAMMATICAL TERMS

ACTIVE The active form of a verb is the basic form as in I *remember* her. It is normally opposed to the **PASSIVE** form of the verb as in she *will be remembered*.

ADJECTIVE An adjective provides supplementary information about a noun, describing what something is like, eg a *small* house, a *red* car, an *interesting* pastime.

ADVERB Adverbs are normally used with a verb to add extra information by indicating *how* the action is done (adverbs of manner), *when*, *where* or *with how much intensity* the action is done (adverbs of time, place and intensity), or *to what extent* the action is done (adverbs of quantity). Adverbs may also be used with an adjective or another adverb, eg a *very* attractive girl, *very* well.

AGREEMENT In French, words such as adjectives, articles and pronouns must agree in number and gender with the noun or pronoun to which they refer. This means that their spelling changes according to the *number* of the noun (singular or plural) and according to its *gender* (masculine or feminine).

ANTECEDENT The antecedent of a relative pronoun is the word or words to which the relative pronoun refers. The antecedent is usually found directly before the relative pronoun, eg in the sentence I know *the man* who did this, *the man* is the antecedent of *who*.

APPOSITION A word or a clause is said to be in apposition to another when it is placed directly after it without any joining word, eg Mr Jones, *our bank manager*, rang today.

ARTICLE *See* DEFINITE ARTICLE, INDEFINITE ARTICLE *and* PARTITIVE ARTICLE.

ASPIRATE H If a word begins with an aspirate h in French, it means that there is no liaison between it and the word preceding it, eg in les haricots the s of les is not pronounced. Similarly, there is no contraction in spelling, eg la haine and not 'l'haine'. *See* SILENT H.

AUXILIARY The French auxiliary verbs are avoir ('to have') and être ('to be'). They are used to make up the first part of compound tenses, the second part being a past participle, eg j'*ai* mangé, il *est* allé.

CARDINAL Cardinal numbers are numbers such as one, two, ten, fourteen, as opposed to ORDINAL numbers, eg first, second.

CLAUSE A clause is a group of words which contains at least a subject and a verb: he said is a clause. A clause often contains more than this basic information, eg he said this to her yesterday. Sentences can be made up of several clauses, eg he said/he'd call me/if he were free. *See* SENTENCE.

COMPARATIVE The comparative forms of adjectives and adverbs allow two things, persons or actions to be compared. In English, more ... than; ... er than; less ... than and as ... as are used for comparison.

COMPLEMENT The complement is the part of the clause which completes the information on the subject. It may be a noun group (That is *a very difficult question*, She'll make *a good leader*), an adjective group (You seem *tired and stressed*) or a prepositional phrase, that is, a preposition plus a noun group (The cat is *in the garden*).

COMPOUND TENSE Compound tenses are verb tenses consisting of more than one element. In French, the compound tenses of a verb are formed by the *auxiliary* verb and the *past participle*: j'ai visité, il est venu.

CONDITIONAL This mood is used to describe what someone would do, or something that would happen if a condition were fulfilled, eg *I would come* if I were well; the chair *would have broken* if he had sat on it.

CONJUGATION The conjugation of a verb is the set of different forms taken in the particular tenses of that verb.

CONJUNCTION Conjunctions are used to link different clauses. They may be coordinating or subordinating. Coordinating conjunctions are words like **and, but, or**, subordinating conjunctions are words like **because, after, although**.

DEFINITE ARTICLE The definite article is **the** in English and **le, la** and **les** in French.

DEMONSTRATIVE Demonstrative adjectives such as **this, that, these** and pronouns such as **this one, that one** are used to point out a particular person or object.

DIRECT OBJECT A direct object is a noun or a pronoun which in English follows a verb without any linking preposition, eg I met *a friend*.

ELISION Elision consists in replacing the last letter of certain words (**le, la, je, me, te, se, de, que**) with an apostrophe before a word starting with a vowel or a **SILENT H**, eg l'eau, l'homme, j'aime.

ENDING The ending of a verb is determined by the *person* (1st/2nd/3rd) and *number* (singular/plural) of its subject. In French, most tenses have six different endings. *See* PERSON *and* NUMBER.

EXCLAMATION An exclamation is a word or sentence used to express surprise or wonder, eg **what!, how!, how lucky!, what a nice day!**

FEMININE *See* GENDER.

GENDER The gender of a noun indicates whether the noun is *masculine* or *feminine* (all French nouns are either masculine or feminine).

IDIOMS Idioms, or idiomatic expressions, are phrases which cannot normally be translated word for word. For example, **it's raining cats and dogs** is translated by il pleut des cordes.

IMPERATIVE This mood is used for giving orders, eg **eat!, don't go!**

INDEFINITE Indefinite pronouns and adjectives are words that do not refer to a definite person or object, eg **each, someone, every.**

INDEFINITE ARTICLE The indefinite article is **a/an** in English and **un, une** and **des** in French.

INDICATIVE The indicative is the 'normal' form of a verb as in **I like, he came, we are trying.** It is used for asking questions and making statements, and is opposed to the subjunctive, conditional and imperative.

INDIRECT OBJECT An indirect object is a pronoun or noun which follows a verb indirectly, with a linking preposition (usually **to**), eg **I spoke to *my friend/him*.**

INFINITIVE The infinitive is the basic form of the verb as found in dictionaries. Thus **to eat** and **to finish** are infinitives. In French, the infinitive is recognizable by its ending (**-er, -ir** or **-re**, eg **manger, finir, prendre**).

INTERROGATIVE Interrogative words are used to ask a question. This may be a direct question (***when* will you arrive?**) or an indirect question (**I don't know *when* he'll arrive**). *See* QUESTION.

MASCULINE *See* GENDER.

MOOD This is the name given to the four main areas within which a verb is conjugated. *See* INDICATIVE, SUBJUNCTIVE, CONDITIONAL, IMPERATIVE.

NOUN A noun is a word or group of words which refers to a living creature, a thing, a place or an abstract idea, eg **postman, cat, shop, passport, life.**

NUMBER The number of a noun indicates whether the noun is *singular* or *plural*. A singular noun refers to one single person or thing, eg **boy, train** and a plural noun to more than one, eg **boys, trains.**

ORDINAL   Ordinal numbers are first, second, third, fourth and all other numbers which end in -th. In French, all ordinal numbers, except for premier ('first') and second ('second'), end in -ième.

PARTITIVE ARTICLE   The partitive articles are some and any in English and du, de la, de l' and des (as in du pain, de la confiture, de l'eau, des bananes) in French.

PASSIVE   A verb is used in the passive when the subject of the verb does not perform the action but is subjected to it. The passive is formed with the verb to be and the past participle of the verb, eg he was rewarded. It is used in contrast to the ACTIVE.

PAST PARTICIPLE   The past participle of a verb is the form which is used after to have in English, eg I have *eaten*; I have *said*; you have *tried*.

PERSON   In any tense, there are three persons in the singular (1st: I ..., 2nd: you ..., 3rd: he/she ...), and three in the plural (1st: we ..., 2nd: you ..., 3rd: they ...). *See also* ENDING.

PERSONAL PRONOUNS   Personal pronouns stand for a noun. They usually accompany a verb and can be either the subject (I, you, he/she/it, we, they) or the object of the verb (me, you, him/her/it, us, them).

PLURAL   *See* NUMBER.

POSSESSIVE   Possessive adjectives and pronouns are used to indicate possession or ownership. They are words like my/mine, your/yours, our/ours.

PREPOSITION   Prepositions are words such as with, in, to, at. They are followed by a noun or a pronoun.

PRESENT PARTICIPLE   The present participle is the verb form which ends in -ing in English and -ant in French.

PRONOUN This is a word which stands for a noun. The main categories of pronouns are:

Relative pronouns (eg who, which, that)

Interrogative pronouns (eg who?, what?, which?)

Demonstrative pronouns (eg this, that, these)

Possessive pronouns (eg mine, yours, his)

Personal pronouns (eg you, him, us)

Reflexive pronouns (eg myself, himself)

Indefinite pronouns (eg something, all)

QUESTION There are two question forms: *direct* questions stand on their own and require a question mark at the end, eg when will he come?; *indirect* questions are introduced by a clause and require no question mark, eg I wonder when he will come.

REFLEXIVE Reflexive verbs 'reflect' the action back onto the subject, eg I dressed myself. They are always found with a reflexive pronoun and are much more common in French than in English.

SENTENCE A sentence is a group of words made up of one or more clauses (*see* CLAUSE) and which makes a complete grammatical structure. The end of a sentence is indicated by a punctuation mark (usually a full stop, a question mark or an exclamation mark).

SILENT H The term 'silent h' is actually misleading since an h is never pronounced in French. The point is that when a silent h occurs, any preceding vowel is not pronounced either. For example, the h in j'habite is silent (note the j'). The h in je hurle, however, is *aspirate*, and so there is no contraction in spelling.

SIMPLE TENSE Simple tenses are tenses in which the verb consists of one word only, eg j'habite, Maurice partira.

SINGULAR *See* NUMBER.

SUBJECT The subject of a verb is the noun or pronoun which performs the action. In the sentences, the train left early and she bought a record, *the train* and *she* are the subjects.

SUBJUNCTIVE   The subjunctive is a verb form which is rarely used in English, eg **if I were you**, **God save the Queen**, but common in French.

SUBORDINATE CLAUSE   A subordinate clause is a group of words with a **SUBJECT** and a **VERB** which is dependent on another clause, ie it cannot stand alone. For example, in **he said he would leave**, *he would leave* is the subordinate clause dependent on *he said*.

SUPERLATIVE   The superlative is the form of an adjective or an adverb which, in English, is marked by **the most ...**, **the ...est** or **the least ...**

TENSE   Verbs are used in tenses, which tell us whether an action takes place in the present, the past or the future.

VERB   A verb is a word which describes the performance of an action, eg **to sing, to work, to watch** or the existence of a state, eg **to be, to have, to hope.**

2 ARTICLES

A THE DEFINITE ARTICLE

1 Forms

In English, there is only one form of the definite article: **the**. In French, there are three forms, depending on the gender and number of the noun following the article:

> ❑ with a masculine singular noun: **le**
> ❑ with a feminine singular noun: **la**　　**the**
> ❑ with a plural noun (masc or fem): **les**

MASC SING	FEM SING	PLURAL
le chauffeur	**la secrétaire**	**les étudiants**
the driver	the secretary	the students
le salon	**la cuisine**	**les chambres**
the living-room	the kitchen	the bedrooms

Note that **le** and **la** both change to **l'** before a vowel or a silent **h**:

	MASCULINE	FEMININE
before vowel	**l'avion**	**l'odeur**
	the plane	the smell
before silent h	**l'homme**	**l'hôtesse**
	the man	the hostess

Pronunciation: the **s** of **les** is pronounced **z** when the noun following it begins with a vowel or a silent **h**.

2 Forms with the prepositions à and de

When the definite article is used with à or de, the following spelling
changes take place:

a) *with* à *(to, at)*

à + le	→	au
à + les	→	aux

à + la and à + l' do not change.

Pronunciation: the x of aux is pronounced z when the noun following it
begins with a vowel or a silent h.

au restaurant
at/to the restaurant

aux enfants
to the children

à la plage
at/to the beach

à l'aéroport
at/to the airport

b) *with* de *(of, from)*

de + le	→	du
de + les	→	des

de + la and de + l' do not change.

Pronunciation: the s of des is pronounced z when the noun following it
begins with a vowel or a silent h.

du directeur
of/from the manager

des chômeurs
of/from the unemployed

de la région
of/from the area

de l'usine
of/from the factory

3 Use

As in English, the definite article is used when referring to a
particular person or thing, or particular persons or things:

les amis dont je t'ai parlé
the friends I told you about

le café est prêt
the coffee is ready

However, the definite article is used far more frequently in French than in English. It is used in particular in the following cases where English uses no article:

a) *when the noun is used in a general sense*

   i) to refer to all things of a kind:

   vous acceptez les chèques?   **le sucre est mauvais pour les dents**
   do you take cheques?   sugar is bad for the teeth

   ii) to refer to abstract things:

   le travail et les loisirs   **la musique classique**
   work and leisure   classical music

   iii) when stating likes and dislikes:

   j'aime le café mais je préfère le thé   **je déteste les tomates**
   I like coffee, but I prefer tea   I hate tomatoes

b) *with geographical names*

   i) continents, countries and areas:

le Canada	**la France**	**l'Europe**
Canada	France	Europe
la Bretagne	**l'Afrique**	**les États-Unis**
Brittany	Africa	the United States

   But: the article la is omitted with the prepositions en and de when used with feminine country names:

   j'habite en France   **il vient d'Italie**
   I live in France   he comes from Italy

   With masculine country names, the corresponding prepositions à and de follow the normal rules:

   j'habite au Portugal/aux États-Unis
   I live in Portugal/in the United States

   je viens du Japon/des Pays-Bas
   I come from Japan/the Netherlands

A very few country names do not require an article, eg Panamá, Cuba, Taïwan, Singapour.

ii) mountains, lakes and rivers:

le mont Everest
Mount Everest

le lac de Genève
Lake Geneva

c) *with names of seasons*

l'automne autumn	**l'hiver** winter
le printemps spring	**l'été** summer
But: **en automne/été/hiver** in autumn/summer/winter	**un jour d'été** a summer's day
au printemps in spring	

d) *with names of languages*

j'apprends le français
I'm learning French

But: **ce film est en anglais**
this film is in English

e) *with parts of the body*

j'ai les cheveux roux
I've got red hair

ouvrez la bouche
open your mouth

les mains en l'air!
hands up!

l'homme à la barbe noire
the man with the black beard

f) *with names following an adjective*

le petit Pierre
little Pierre

la pauvre Isabelle
poor Isabelle

g) *with titles*
le docteur Coste   **le commandant Cousteau**
Doctor Coste   Captain Cousteau

h) *with days of the week to express regular occurrences*

que fais-tu le samedi?
what do you do on Saturdays?

le docteur reçoit le lundi et le vendredi
the doctor sees patients on Mondays and Fridays

i) *with names of subjects or leisure activities*
les maths   **l'histoire et la géographie**
maths   history and geography

la natation, la lecture, le football
swimming, reading, football

j) *in expressions of price, quantity etc*
c'est combien le kilo/la douzaine/la bouteille?
how much is it for a kilo/dozen/bottle?

B THE INDEFINITE ARTICLE

1 Forms

In French, there are three forms of the indefinite article, depending
on the number and gender of the noun it accompanies:

❏ with a masculine singular noun:	un	a
❏ with a feminine singular noun:	une	a
❏ with a plural noun (masc or fem):	des	some

Note

Des is often not translated in English:
il y a des nuages dans le ciel
there are clouds in the sky

2 Use

a) On the whole, the French indefinite article is used in the same way as its English equivalent:

un homme	**une femme**	**des hommes/femmes**
a man	a woman	(some) men/women
un livre	**une tasse**	**des livres/tasses**
a book	a cup	(some) books/cups

b) However, the English indefinite article is not always translated in French:

 i) when stating someone's profession or occupation:

mon père est architecte	**elle est médecin**
my father is an architect	she is a doctor

Note, however, that the article is used after c'est, c'était *etc*:

c'est un acteur célèbre	**ce sont des fraises**
he's a famous actor	these are strawberries

 ii) with nouns in apposition:

Madame Leclerc, employée de bureau
Mrs Leclerc, an office worker

 iii) after quel in exclamations:

quel dommage!	**quelle surprise!**
what a pity!	what a surprise!

c) In negative sentences, de (or d') is used instead of un, une, des:

je n'ai pas d'amis	**je n'ai plus de voiture**
I don't have any friends	I don't have a car any more

d) In French (but not in English), the indefinite article is used with abstract nouns followed by an adjective:

avec une patience remarquable
with remarkable patience

elle a fait des progrès étonnants
she's made amazing progress

Note, however, that the article is not used when there is no adjective:

avec plaisir	**sans hésitation**
with pleasure	without hesitation

C THE PARTITIVE ARTICLE

1 Forms

There are three forms of the French partitive article, which corresponds to 'some'/'any' in English:

> ❑ with a masculine singular noun: **du**
> ❑ with a feminine singular noun: **de la**
> ❑ with plural nouns (masc or fem):   **des**

du vin	**de la bière**	**des fruits**
some wine	some beer	some fruit

Note that de l' is used in front of masculine or feminine singular nouns beginning with a vowel or a silent h:

de l'argent	**de l'eau**
some money	some water
de l'hélium	
some helium	

2 Use

a) On the whole, the French partitive article is used as in English. However, English tends to omit the partitive article where French does not:

achète du pain	**vous avez du beurre?**
buy (some) bread	do you have (any) butter?
je voudrais de la viande	**tu veux de la soupe?**
I'd like some meat	do you want (any) soup?
tu dois manger des légumes	**as-tu acheté des poires?**
you must eat (some) vegetables	did you buy any pears?

b) The partitive article is replaced by de (or d') in the following cases:

   i) in negative expressions:

il n'y a plus de café there isn't any coffee left	**je n'ai pas d'enfants** I don't have any children
nous n'avons plus d'argent we don't have any money left	**je n'ai pas de frères** I don't have any brothers

Note, however, that when the clause is introduced by c'est, il est *etc*, the partitive article remains:

ce n'est pas du cuir, c'est du plastique
it's not leather, it's plastic

   ii) after expressions of quantity (*see also* pp 227-9):

il boit trop de café he drinks too much coffee	**il gagne assez d'argent** he earns enough money

   iii) after avoir besoin de:

j'ai besoin d'argent I need (some) money	**tu as besoin de timbres?** do you need (any) stamps?

   iv) where an adjective is followed by a plural noun:

de petites villes (some) small towns	**d'énormes mensonges** outrageous lies

Note, however, that if the adjective comes after the noun, des does not change:

des résultats encourageants
encouraging results

2 Partitive or definite article?

When no article is used in English, it is not always clear which is the right article in French: le/la/les or du/de la/des.

If **some/any** can be inserted before the English noun, the French partitive article should be used. But if the noun is used in a general sense and inserting **some/any** in front of the English noun does not make sense, the definite article must be used:

did you buy fish? (= *any fish*)
tu as acheté du poisson?

yes, I did; I like fish (= *fish in general*)
oui; j'aime le poisson

3 NOUNS

A noun is a word or group of words which refers to a person, an animal, a thing, a place or an abstract idea.

A GENDER

All French nouns are either masculine or feminine; there is no neuter as in English. Though *no absolute rule can be stated*, the gender can often be determined either by the meaning or the ending of the noun.

1 Masculine

a) *by meaning*

   i) words referring to men and male animals:

un homme	**le boucher**	**le tigre**
a man	the butcher	the tiger

   ii) names of common trees and shrubs:

le chêne	**le sapin**	**le laurier**
the oak	the fir tree	the laurel

   iii) days, months, seasons:

lundi	**mars**	**le printemps**
Monday	March	spring

   iv) languages:

le français	**le polonais**	**le russe**
French	Polish	Russian

   v) rivers and countries not ending in a silent e:

le Nil	**le Portugal**	**le Danemark**
the Nile	Portugal	Denmark

Note, however, that there are exceptions to this rule:

le Danube	le Rhône	le Mexique
the Danube	the Rhone	Mexico

b) *by ending*

-acle	le spectacle (show)
	But: une débâcle (shambles)
-age	le fromage (cheese)
	But: la cage (cage), une image (picture), la nage (swimming), la page (page), la plage (beach), la rage (rage, rabies)
-é	le marché (market)
	But: nouns ending in -té and -tié are usually feminine (*see* p 28)
-eau	le chapeau (hat)
	But: l'eau (water), la peau (skin)
-ège	le piège (trap), le collège (secondary school)
-ème	le thème (theme, topic)
	But: la crème (cream)
-isme, -asme	le communisme (communism), le tourisme (tourism), l'enthousiasme (enthusiasm)
-o	le numéro (the number)
	But: la dynamo (dynamo) and most abbreviated expressions: une auto (car), la météo (weather forecast), la photo (photograph), la radio (radio), la sténo (shorthand), la stéréo (stereo)

Nouns ending in a *consonant* are usually *masculine*.

Notable exceptions are:

i) most nouns ending in -tion, -sion, -ation, -aison, -ison

ii) most abstract nouns ending in -eur (*see* p 28)

iii) the following nouns ending in a consonant:

la clef (key)	la nef (nave)
la soif (thirst)	la faim (hunger)
la fin (end)	la façon (manner)
la leçon (lesson)	la boisson (drink)
la moisson (harvest)	la rançon (ransom)
la mer (sea)	la cuiller (spoon)
la chair (flesh)	la basse-cour (farmyard)
la cour (yard)	la tour (tower)
la brebis (ewe)	une fois (once)
la vis (screw)	la souris (mouse)
la part (share)	la plupart (majority, most)
la dent (tooth)	la dot (dowry)
la forêt (forest)	la jument (mare)
la mort (death)	la nuit (night)
la croix (cross)	la noix (nut)
la paix (peace)	la perdrix (partridge)
la toux (cough)	la voix (voice)

2 Feminine

a) *by meaning*

i) words referring to women and female animals:

la mère	la bonne	la génisse
the mother	the maid	the heifer

ii) names of rivers and countries ending with a silent e:

la Seine	la Russie	la Belgique
the Seine	Russia	Belgium

iii) saints' days and festivals:

la Toussaint	la Pentecôte
All Saints' Day	Whitsun

Note, however, that Noël (Christmas) is masculine except when used with the definite article: à la Noël (at Christmas).

b) *by ending*

-ace	la place (square, seat)
	But: un espace (space)
-ade	la salade (salad)
	But: le grade (degree, rank), le stade (stadium)
-ance, -anse	la puissance (power), la danse (dancing)
-ée	la soirée (evening), la journée (day)
	But: le musée (museum), le lycée (secondary school)
-ence, -ense	une évidence (evidence), la défense (defence)
	But: le silence (silence)
-ère	la lumière (light)
	But: le mystère (mystery), le caractère (character)
-eur	la peur (fear)
	But: le bonheur (happiness), le chœur (choir), le cœur (heart), un honneur (honour), le labeur (toil), le malheur (misfortune)
-ie	la pluie (rain)
	But: le génie (genius), un incendie (fire), le parapluie (umbrella)
-ière	la bière (beer)
	But: le cimetière (cemetery)
-oire	la gloire (glory)
	But: le laboratoire (laboratory), le pourboire (tip)
-tion, -sion, -ation, -aison, -ison	la fiction (fiction), la nation (nation), la raison (reason), la prison (prison)
-té	la bonté (goodness)
	But: le côté (side), le comté (county), le traité (treaty), le pâté (pâté)
-tié	la moitié (half), la pitié (pity)

Most nouns ending in a silent e following two consonants are feminine:

> **la botte** (boot), **la couronne** (crown), **la terre** (earth), **la masse** (mass), **la lutte** (struggle)

But: **le verre** (glass), **le parterre** (flower-bed), **le tonnerre** (thunder), **un intervalle** (interval), **le carrosse** (carriage)

3 Difficulties

a) Some nouns may have either gender depending on the sex of the person to whom they refer:

un artiste a (male) artist	**une artiste** a (female) artist
le Russe the Russian (man)	**la Russe** the Russian (woman)

similarly:

un aide/une aide an assistant	**un camarade/une camarade** a friend
un domestique/une domestique a servant	**un enfant/une enfant** a child
un malade/une malade a patient	**un propriétaire/une propriétaire** an owner

b) Others have only one gender for both sexes:

un ange an angel	**un amateur** an enthusiast	**un auteur** an author
une connaissance an acquaintance	**une dupe** a dupe	**un écrivain** a writer
une personne a person	**le médecin** the doctor	**le peintre** the painter
la recrue the recruit	**le sculpteur** the sculptor	**la sentinelle** the sentry
le témoin the witness	**la victime** the victim	**la vedette** the (film) star

Note, however, that modern French tends to use feminine forms for many different functions. La ministre, la juge and la professeur can now be commonly found in the press, and new forms such as une écrivaine have also begun to appear.

c) The following nouns change meaning according to gender:

	MASCULINE	FEMININE
aide	male assistant	assistance; female assistant
crêpe	mourning band	pancake
critique	critic	criticism
faux	forgery	scythe
livre	book	pound
manche	handle	sleeve
manœuvre	labourer	manoeuvre
mémoire	memorandum	memory
mode	method, way	fashion
mort	dead man	death
moule	mould	mussel
page	pageboy	page
pendule	pendulum	clock
physique	physique	physics
poêle	stove	frying pan
poste	post (*job*), set	post office
somme	nap	sum
tour	trick, tour	tower
trompette	trumpeter	trumpet
vapeur	steamer	steam
vase	vase	silt
voile	veil	sail

d) A few words vary in gender according to their usage. The plural noun gens is regarded as feminine when it follows an adjective, and masculine when it precedes it:

de bonnes gens   **des gens ennuyeux**
good people   boring people

The words amour, délice and orgue are masculine when used in the singular and feminine when used in the plural:

un amour de jeunesse   **des amours malheureuses**
an old flame   unhappy love affairs
un délice inoubliable   **des délices infinies**
an unforgettable delight   infinite delights
un orgue électrique   **les grandes orgues**
an electric organ   the great organ

e) *City names*
Some city names are traditionally feminine:

La Rochelle   **La Haye**   **Alger la Blanche**
La Rochelle   The Hague   Algiers, the white city

Others are masculine in everyday usage:

le Paris des années 30   **le vieux Nice**
Paris in the 30s   old Nice

le Londres de mon souvenir   **Berlin fut totalement détruit**
the London I remember   Berlin was completely destroyed

In literary French, however, city names are feminine:

Caen fut prise après de terribles bombardements
Caen was taken after a terrible bombardment

B THE FORMATION OF FEMININES

The feminine of nouns may be formed in the following ways:

1 By adding an **e** to the masculine form:

un ami	**une amie**
a (male) friend	a (female) friend
un Hollandais	**une Hollandaise**
a Dutchman	a Dutch woman

Note that nouns which end in -e in the masculine form do not change:

un élève	**une élève**
a (male) pupil	a (female) pupil

Note also that the addition of an **e** often entails an alteration of the masculine form:

a) nouns ending in -t and -n double the final consonant:

le chien/la chienne	**le chat/la chatte**
dog/bitch	cat

b) nouns ending in -er add a grave accent to the **e** immediately preceding the r:

un ouvrier/une ouvrière
workman/female worker

c) nouns ending in -eur change into –euse, or in some cases -eresse:

le vendeur/la vendeuse	**le pécheur/la pécheresse**
male/female shop assistant	sinner

d) nouns ending in -teur change into -teuse or -trice according to the following guidelines:

if the stem of the word is also that of a present participle the feminine form ends in -euse:

le chanteur/la chanteuse
male/female singer

if the stem is not that of a present participle, the feminine form ends in -trice:

le lecteur/la lectrice
male/female reader

e) nouns ending in -f change into -ve:

le veuf/la veuve
widower/widow

f) nouns ending in -x change into -se:

un époux/une épouse
husband/wife

g) nouns ending in -eau change into -elle:

le jumeau/la jumelle
male/female twin

2 By using a different word (as in English):

le beau-fils/la belle-fille	son-/daughter-in-law
le beau-père/la belle-mère	father-/mother-in-law
le bélier/la brebis	ram/ewe
le bœuf/la vache	ox/cow
le canard/la cane	drake/duck
le cheval/la jument	horse/mare
le cerf/la biche	stag/hind
le coq/la poule	cock/hen
le fils/la fille	son/daughter
le frère/la sœur	brother/sister

un homme/une femme	man/woman
un jars/une oie	gander/goose
le mâle/la femelle	male/female
le neveu/la nièce	nephew/niece
un oncle/une tante	uncle/aunt
le parrain/la marraine	godfather/godmother
le père/la mère	father/mother
le porc/la truie	pig/sow
le roi/la reine	king/queen

3 By adding the word femme (or femelle for animals):

une femme médecin	un perroquet femelle
doctor	female parrot

4 Irregular feminine forms

un abbé/une abbesse	abbot/abbess
un âne/une ânesse	donkey
le comte/la comtesse	count/countess
le dieu/la déesse	god/goddess
le duc/la duchesse	duke/duchess
un Esquimau/une Esquimaude	Eskimo
le fou/la folle	madman/mad woman
un Grec/une Grecque	Greek
un héros/une héroïne	hero/heroine
un hôte/une hôtesse	host/hostess
le maître/la maîtresse	master/mistress
le prêtre/la prêtresse	priest/priestess
le prince/la princesse	prince/princess
le tigre/la tigresse	tiger/tigress
le Turc/la Turque	Turk
le vieux/la vieille	old man/old woman

C THE FORMATION OF PLURALS

1 Most nouns form their plural by adding **s** to the singular:

| le vin | les vins | wine(s) |
| un étudiant | des étudiants | student(s) |

2 Nouns ending in -**s**, -**x** or -**z** remain unchanged:

le bras	les bras	arm(s)
la voix	les voix	voice(s)
le nez	les nez	nose(s)

3 Nouns ending in -**au**, -**eau** and -**eu** add **x** to the singular:

	le tuyau	les tuyaux	drainpipe(s)
	le bateau	les bateaux	boat(s)
	le jeu	les jeux	game(s)
But:	le landau	les landaus	pram(s)
	le bleu	les bleus	bruise(s)
	le pneu	les pneus	tyre(s)

4 Nouns ending in -**al** change to -**aux**:

	le journal	les journaux	newspaper(s)
But:	le bal	les bals	dance(s)
	le carnaval	les carnavals	carnival(s)
	le festival	les festivals	festival(s)

5 Nouns ending in -**ail** change to -**aux**:

	le bail	les baux	lease(s)
	le travail	les travaux	work(s)
	le vitrail	les vitraux	stained-glass window(s)
But:	le détail	les détails	detail(s)
	l'épouvantail	les épouvantails	scarecrow(s)
	l'éventail	les éventails	fan(s)
	le rail	les rails	rail(s)

6 Nouns ending in -ou:

a) Seven nouns ending in -ou add x in the plural:

le bijou	les bijoux	jewel(s)
le caillou	les cailloux	pebble(s)
le chou	les choux	cabbage(s)
le genou	les genoux	knee(s)
le hibou	les hiboux	owl(s)
le joujou	les joujoux	toy(s)
le pou	les poux	louse (lice)

b) Other nouns ending in -ou add s:

le clou	les clous	nail(s)

7 Plural of compound nouns:

Each noun ought to be checked individually in a dictionary:

	le chou-fleur	les choux-fleurs	cauliflower(s)
	le beau-père	les beaux-pères	father(s)-in-law
But:	un essuie-glace	des essuie-glaces	windscreen wiper(s)
	le tire-bouchon	les tire-bouchons	corkscrew(s)

8 Irregular plurals:

un œil	des yeux	eye(s)
le ciel	les cieux	sky (skies)
Monsieur	Messieurs	Mr (Gentlemen)
Madame	Mesdames	Mrs (Ladies)
Mademoiselle	Mesdemoiselles	Miss (Ladies)

9 Collective nouns:

a) Some nouns are singular in French but plural in English:

le bétail	la recette	la police
cattle	takings	police

la police a arrêté certains grévistes
the police *have* arrested some strikers

b) Others are plural in French but singular in English:

le nouvelles	**les capitaux**	**les cheveux**
news	capital	hair

les nouvelles sont bonnes
the news *is* good

10 Proper nouns:

a) Ordinary family names are invariable:

j'ai rencontré les Leblanc
I met the Leblancs

b) Historical names add -s:

les Stuarts	**les Bourbons**	**les Tudors**
the Stuarts	the Bourbons	the Tudors

4 ADJECTIVES

Adjectives usually accompany a noun (or a pronoun) and provide extra information about what someone or something is like:

une grande ville	**un passe-temps** intéressant
a *large* city	an *interesting* pastime
elle est espagnole	**c'était** ennuyeux
she is *Spanish*	it was *boring*

 A AGREEMENT OF ADJECTIVES

In French, adjectives agree in number and gender with the noun or pronoun to which they refer. This means that French adjectives have four different forms which are determined by the noun they accompany:

❏ **masculine singular** (basic form, found in the dictionary)
❏ **feminine singular**
❏ **masculine plural**
❏ **feminine plural**

un passeport vert	**une voiture** verte
a green passport	a green car
des gants verts	**des chaussettes** vertes
green gloves	green socks

Note that if two singular words share the same adjective, the adjective will be in the plural:

un foulard et un bonnet rouges
a red scarf and (a red) hat

If one of these words is feminine and the other masculine, the adjective will be in the masculine plural:

une robe et un manteau noirs
a black dress and (a black) coat

B FEMININE FORMS OF ADJECTIVES

1 General rule

Add the letter e to the masculine singular form:

MASCULINE	FEMININE
grand	grande
amusant	amusante
anglais	anglaise
bronzé	bronzée
un livre amusant	une histoire amusante
an amusing book	an amusing story
il est bronzé	elle est bronzée
he is suntanned	she is suntanned

2 Adjectives already ending in -e

These do not change:

MASCULINE	FEMININE
rouge	rouge
jeune	jeune
malade	malade
mon père est malade	ma mère est malade
my father is ill	my mother is ill

3 Others

The spelling of some adjectives changes when the e is added:

a) The following masculine endings generally double the final consonant before adding e:

MASCULINE ENDING	FEMININE ENDING
-el	-elle
-eil	-eille
-en	-enne
-on	-onne
-as	-asse
-et	-ette

ADJECTIVES

MASCULINE	FEMININE	
réel	réelle	real
cruel	cruelle	cruel
pareil	pareille	similar
ancien	ancienne	old
italien	italienne	Italian
bon	bonne	good
gras	grasse	greasy
bas	basse	low
muet	muette	dumb
net	nette	clear

un problème actuel — la vie actuelle
a topical problem — present-day life

un bon conseil — c'est une bonne recette
good advice — it's a good recipe

Note, however, that the feminine ending of some common adjectives in -et is -ète instead of -ette:

MASCULINE	FEMININE	
complet	complète	complete
incomplet	incomplète	incomplete
concret	concrète	concrete
discret	discrète	discreet
inquiet	inquiète	worried
secret	secrète	secret

b)

MASCULINE -er	FEMININE -ère	
cher	chère	dear
fier	fière	proud
dernier	dernière	last

c)

MASCULINE -x	FEMININE -se	
heureux	heureuse	happy
malheureux	malheureuse	unhappy
sérieux	sérieuse	serious
jaloux	jalouse	jealous
But: doux	douce	soft
faux	fausse	false
roux	rousse	red-haired
vieux	vieille	old

d)

MASCULINE -eur	FEMININE -euse	
menteur	menteuse	lying
trompeur	trompeuse	deceitful

This rule, however, applies only when the stem of the adjective is also the stem of a present participle (eg mentant, trompant). The following five adjectives simply add an e to the feminine:

MASCULINE -eur	FEMININE -eure	
extérieur	extérieure	external
intérieur	intérieure	internal
inférieur	inférieure	inferior
supérieur	supérieure	superior
meilleur	meilleure	better

The feminine ending of the remaining adjectives in -teur is -trice:

MASCULINE	FEMININE	
protecteur	protectrice	protective
destructeur	destructrice	destructive

e)

MASCULINE -f	FEMININE -ve	
neuf	neuve	new
vif	vive	lively
naïf	naïve	naive
actif	active	active
passif	passive	passive
positif	positive	positive
bref	brève (note the è)	brief

f)

MASCULINE -c	FEMININE -che/que	
blanc	blanche	white
franc	franche	frank
sec	sèche	dry
public	publique	public
turc	turque	Turkish
grec	grecque	Greek

g) The following five common adjectives have an irregular feminine form and two forms for the masculine singular; the second masculine form, based on the feminine form, is used before words starting with a vowel or a silent h:

MASC	FEM	MASC 2	
beau	belle	bel	beautiful
nouveau	nouvelle	nouvel	new
vieux	vieille	vieil	old
fou	folle	fol	mad
mou	molle	mol	soft

un beau lac	une belle vue	un bel enfant
a beautiful lake	a beautiful view	a beautiful child
un nouveau disque	la nouvelle année	un nouvel ami
a new record	the new year	a new friend
un vieux tableau	la vieille ville	un vieil homme
an old painting	the old town	an old man

h) Other irregular feminines:

MASCULINE	FEMININE	
favori	favorite	favourite
gentil	gentille	nice
nul	nulle	no
frais	fraîche	fresh
malin	maligne	shrewd
sot	sotte	foolish
long	longue	long
aigu	aiguë	sharp
ambigu	ambiguë	ambiguous
chic	chic	elegant
châtain	châtain	chestnut

C PLURALS OF ADJECTIVES

1 General rule

The masculine and feminine plural of adjectives is formed by adding an s to the singular form:

un vélo neuf	**des vélos neufs**
a new bike	new bikes
une belle fleur	**de belles fleurs**
a beautiful flower	beautiful flowers
le livre intéressant	**les livres intéressants**
the interesting book	the interesting books

2 Adjectives ending in -s or -x

If the masculine singular ends in -s or -x, the plural form does not take an s:

il est heureux	**ils sont heureux**
he's happy	they are happy
un touriste anglais	**des touristes anglais**
an English tourist	English tourists

3 Others

A few masculine plurals are irregular (the feminine plurals are all regular):

a)

	SINGULAR -al	PLURAL -aux	
	normal	normaux	normal
	brutal	brutaux	brutal
	loyal	loyaux	loyal
But:	fatal	fatals	fatal
	natal	natals	native
	naval	navals	naval

Note that the adjective final (final) has two masculine plural forms: **finals** and **finaux**.

b)

SINGULAR -eau	PLURAL -eaux	
beau	beaux	beautiful
nouveau	nouveaux	new

D POSITION OF ADJECTIVES

1 Unlike English adjectives, French adjectives usually follow the noun:

un métier intéressant   **des parents modernes**
an interesting job   modern parents

Adjectives of colour and nationality always follow the noun:

des chaussures rouges   **le drapeau britannique**
red shoes   the British flag

2 However, the following common adjectives generally come before the noun:

beau	beautiful
bon	good
court	short
gentil	nice
grand	big, tall
gros	fat
haut	high
jeune	young
joli	pretty
long	long
mauvais	bad
méchant	nasty, naughty
meilleur	better
moindre	lesser, least
petit	small
pire	worse
vieux	old
vilain	nasty, ugly

3 Some adjectives have a different meaning according to their position:

	BEFORE NOUN	AFTER NOUN
ancien	former	ancient
brave	good	brave
certain	some	sure
cher	dear	expensive
dernier	last (*final*)	last (*latest*)
grand	great (*people only*)	big, tall
même	same	very
pauvre	poor (*pitiable*)	poor (*not rich*)
propre	own	clean
seul	single, only	alone, lonely
simple	mere	simple
vrai	real	true

mon ancien métier
my former job

un tableau ancien
an old painting

un brave type
a nice guy

un homme brave
a brave man

un certain charme
a certain charm

un fait certain
a definite fact

chère Brigitte
dear Brigitte

un cadeau cher
an expensive present

la dernière séance
the last performance

le mois dernier
last month

une grande œuvre d'art
a great work of art

un homme assez grand
quite a tall man

le même endroit
the same place

la vérité même
the truth itself

mon pauvre ami!
my poor friend!

des gens pauvres
poor people

mon propre frère
my own brother

une chambre propre
a clean room

mon seul espoir my only hope	**un homme seul** a lonely man
un simple employé an ordinary employee	**des goûts simples** simple tastes
un vrai casse-pieds a real bore	**une histoire vraie** a true story

If a noun is accompanied by several adjectives, the same rules apply to each of them:

le bon vieux temps the good old days	**un joli foulard rouge** a pretty red scarf

E COMPARATIVE AND SUPERLATIVE OF ADJECTIVES

Persons or things can be compared by using:

1. *the comparative form of the adjective:*

   more ... than
   ...er than
   less ... than
   not as ... as
   as ... as

2. *the superlative form of the adjective:*

   the most ...
   the ...est
   the least ...

1 The comparative

The French comparative is formed as follows:

plus ... (que)	plus long	plus cher
more ... (than)	longer	more expensive
...er (than)		
moins ... (que)	moins long	moins récent
less ... (than)	less long	less recent
not as ... (as)		
aussi ... (que)	aussi bon	aussi important
as ... (as)	as good	as important

une plus grande maison
a larger house

un village plus ancien
an older village

le football est-il plus populaire que le rugby?
is football more popular than rugby?

ces gants sont moins chauds que les autres
these gloves are less warm than the other ones

elle est beaucoup/bien moins patiente que lui
she's far less patient than he is

le problème de la pollution est tout aussi grave
the pollution problem is just as serious

2 The superlative

a) *Formation*

le/la/les plus ...	the most ..., the ...est
le/la/les moins ...	the least ...

le plus grand pays
the largest country

la plus grande ville
the largest city

les plus grands acteurs
the greatest actors

les plus grandes voitures
the largest cars

b) *Word order*

i) The normal rules governing word order of adjectives apply. When a superlative adjective comes after the noun, the article is used twice, before the noun and before the adjective:

le plat le plus délicieux   **l'histoire la plus passionnante**
the most delicious dish   the most exciting story

ii) When a possessive adjective is used, there are two possible constructions, depending on the position of the adjective:

ma plus forte matière
my best subject

or:

mon besoin le plus urgent est de trouver un emploi
my most urgent need is to find a job

c) *'in' is normally translated by* de*:*

la plus jolie maison du quartier/de la ville
the prettiest house in the area/town

le restaurant le plus cher de France
the most expensive restaurant in France

Note that verbs following the superlative usually take the subjunctive (*see* p 135).

3 Irregular comparatives and superlatives

ADJECTIVE	COMPARATIVE	SUPERLATIVE
bon	meilleur	le meilleur
good	better	best
mauvais	pire	le pire
bad	plus mauvais	le plus mauvais
	worse	the worst
petit	moindre	le moindre
small	plus petit	le plus petit
	smaller, lesser	the smallest, the least

Note that pire and le pire are, strictly speaking, the correct comparative and superlative forms of mauvais. Plus mauvais and le plus mauvais can also be found in everyday French, however, with a slight difference in meaning: pire and le pire express the absolute (ie one cannot conceive of a worse example of ...) while plus mauvais and le plus mauvais indicate a comparison of a lesser degree:

il n'y a pas de pire professeur que lui
he is the worst teacher of all

c'est la pire chose qui pouvait lui arriver
it's the worst thing that could happen to him

ma note est plus mauvaise que la tienne
my mark is worse than yours

c'est le plus mauvais élève de la classe
he's the worst pupil in the class

Note, too, that moindre usually means 'less in importance', and plus petit 'less in size':

le moindre de mes soucis   **elle est plus petite que moi**
the least of my worries   she is smaller than I (am)

 F ADJECTIVES OF NATIONALITY

1 French, unlike English, does not use capital letters for adjectives of nationality. Only nouns indicating nationality are written with a capital letter in French:

une voiture anglaise   **une Anglaise**
an English car   an English woman

2 An adjective of nationality in English is sometimes best translated by a genitive construction in French:

l'ambassade de France
the French embassy

l'équipe de Nantes
the Nantes team

le championnat de France
the French league

la Grand Prix du Brésil
the Brazilian Grand Prix

la couronne de France
the French crown

une grammaire de l'anglais
an English grammar

l'équipe de France de rugby
the French rugby team

l'équipe de Glasgow
the Glasgow/Glaswegian team

la Coupe de France de football
the French football cup

la terre de France
French soil

les côtes de France
the French coastline

5 ADVERBS

Adverbs are normally used with a verb to express:

			ADVERBS OF
how			manner
when		an action is done	time
where			place
with how much intensity			intensity
to what extent			quantity

A ADVERBS OF MANNER

These are usually formed by adding -ment to the adjective
(like -ly in English):

1 If the adjective ends in a consonant, -ment is added to its
feminine form:

ADJECTIVE (masc, fem)	ADVERB
doux, douce (soft)	doucement (softly)
franc, franche (frank)	franchement (frankly)
final, finale (final)	finalement (finally)

2 If the adjective ends in a vowel, -ment is added to its
masculine form:

	ADJECTIVE	ADVERB
	absolu (absolute)	absolument (absolutely)
	désespéré (desperate)	désespérément (desperately)
	vrai (true)	vraiment (truly)
	simple (simple)	simplement (simply)
But:	gai (cheerful)	gaiement *or* gaîment (cheerfully)
	nouveau (new)	nouvellement (newly)
	fou (mad)	follement (madly)

3 Many adverbs have irregular forms:

a) Some change the **e** of the feminine form of the adjective to **é** before adding -ment:

ADJECTIVE	ADVERB
commun (common)	**communément** (commonly)
précis (precise)	**précisément** (precisely)
profond (deep)	**profondément** (deeply)
énorme (enormous)	**énormément** (enormously)
aveugle (blind)	**aveuglément** (blindly)

b) Adjectives which end in -ent and -ant change to -emment and -amment. Note that both endings are pronounced like amant:

	ADJECTIVE	ADVERB
	prudent (careful)	**prudemment** (carefully)
	évident (obvious)	**évidemment** (obviously)
	brillant (brilliant)	**brillamment** (brilliantly)
But:	**lent** (slow)	**lentement** (slowly)

4 Some adverbs are completely irregular, including some of the most commonly used ones:

ADJECTIVE	ADVERB
bon (good)	**bien** (well)
bref (brief)	**brièvement** (briefly)
gentil (kind)	**gentiment** (kindly)
mauvais (bad)	**mal** (badly)
meilleur (better)	**mieux** (better)

5 Some adjectives are also used as adverbs in certain set expressions:

parler bas/haut *or* fort	to speak softly/loudly
coûter/payer cher	to cost/pay a lot
s'arrêter net	to stop short
couper court	to cut short
voir clair	to see clearly
marcher droit	to walk straight
travailler dur	to work hard
chanter faux/juste	to sing off key/in tune
sentir mauvais/bon	to smell bad/good
refuser net	to refuse point blank

6 After verbs relating to saying something or looking at something in French an adverbial phrase is often preferred to an adverb:

'tu m'écriras?' dit-il d'une voix triste
'will you write to me?' he said *sadly*

elle nous a regardés d'un air dédaigneux
she looked at us *disdainfully*

7 English adverbs may be expressed in French by a preposition followed by a noun:

sans soin	avec fierté	avec amour
carelessly	proudly	lovingly

B ADVERBS OF TIME

These are not usually formed from adjectives. The commonest ones are the following:

alors	then
après	afterwards
aujourd'hui	today
aussitôt	at once
bientôt	soon
d'abord	first
déjà	already
demain	tomorrow
encore	still, again
pas encore	not yet
enfin	at last, finally
hier	yesterday
parfois	sometimes
rarement	seldom
souvent	often
tard	late
tôt	early
toujours	always
tout de suite	immediately

c'est déjà Noël!
it's Christmas already!

tu as déjà essayé?
have you tried before?

il mange encore!
he's still eating!

elle n'est pas encore arrivée
she hasn't arrived yet

C ADVERBS OF PLACE

Like adverbs of time, these are not usually formed from adjectives. The commonest ones are the following:

ailleurs	elsewhere	**au-dessous**	below
ici	here	**dedans**	inside
là	there	**dehors**	outside
loin	far away	**devant**	in front, ahead
dessus	on top, on it	**derrière**	behind
au-dessus	over, above	**partout**	everywhere
dessous	underneath		

ne restez pas dehors!
don't stay outside!

qu'est-ce qu'il y a dedans?
what's inside?

mon nom est marqué dessus
my name is written on it

passez devant
go in front

 D ADVERBS OF INTENSITY AND QUANTITY

These may be used with a verb, an adjective or another adverb. The commonest ones are the following:

à peine	hardly	**peu**	little
assez	enough, quite	**seulement**	only
autant	as much/many	**si**	so
beaucoup	a lot, much/many	**tant**	so much/many
combien	how much/many	**tellement**	so much/many
comme	how	**très**	very
moins	less	**trop**	too (much/many)
plus	more	**un peu**	a little
presque	nearly		

vous avez assez bu!
you've had enough to drink!

nous avons beaucoup ri
we laughed a lot

je vais un peu mieux
I'm feeling a little better

elle parle trop
she talks too much

il ne fait pas assez chaud
it's not warm enough

comme c'est amusant!
how funny!

c'est si fatigant!
it's so tiring!

il est très timide
he's very shy

Note that all of these adverbs, except à peine, comme, presque, si, très and seulement, may be followed by de and a noun to express a quantity (*see* pp 227–8).

E POSITION OF ADVERBS

1 Adverbs usually follow verbs:

je vais rarement au théâtre
I seldom go to the theatre

comme vous conduisez prudemment!
you do drive carefully!

2 With compound tenses, shorter adverbs usually come between the auxiliary and the past participle:

j'ai enfin terminé
I have finished at last

il me l'a déjà dit
he's already told me

nous y sommes souvent allés
we've often gone there

elle avait beaucoup souffert
she had suffered a lot

3 Adverbs of place and many adverbs of time, however, follow the past participle:

je l'ai rencontré hier
I met him yesterday

mettez-le dehors
put it outside

elle avait cherché partout
she had looked everywhere

tu t'es couché tard?
did you go to bed late?

4 Adverbs usually come before adjectives or other adverbs, as in English:

très rarement
very seldom

trop vite
too quickly

elle est vraiment belle
she is really beautiful

 **COMPARATIVE AND SUPERLATIVE OF ADVERBS**

1 The comparative and superlative of adverbs are formed in the same way as those of adjectives:

ADVERB	COMPARATIVE	SUPERLATIVE
souvent often	plus souvent (que) more often (than)	le plus souvent (the) most often
	aussi souvent (que) as often (as)	
	moins souvent (que) less often (than) not as often (as)	le moins souvent (the) least often

Note that the superlative of the adverb always takes the masculine singular article **le**:

je le vois plus souvent qu'avant
I see him more often than I used to

il conduit moins prudemment que moi
he drives less carefully than I do
he doesn't drive as carefully as I do

c'est lui qui conduit le moins prudemment
he's the one who drives the least carefully

je sais cuisiner aussi bien que toi!
I can cook as well as you!

> *Note*
>
> - Expressions with 'as ... as possible' are translated either by
>   aussi ... que possible or by le plus ... possible:
>
>   as far as possible   **aussi loin que possible**
>   **le plus loin possible**
>
> - After a negative, aussi is often replaced by si:
>
>   **pas si vite!**
>   not so fast!
>
> - In French, the idea of 'not so' or 'not as' is often expressed by
>   moins ('less'):
>
>   **parle moins fort!**
>   don't talk so loud!

2 Irregular comparatives and superlatives

ADVERB	COMPARATIVE	SUPERLATIVE
beaucoup	**plus**	**le plus**
much, a lot	more	(the) most
bien	**mieux**	**le mieux**
well	better	(the) best
mal	**pis** *or* **plus mal**	**le pis** *or* **le plus mal**
badly	worse	(the) worst
peu	**moins**	**le moins**
little	less	(the) least

il est mieux payé que moi   **c'est lui le mieux payé**
he is better paid than me   he's the best paid

Note

• Mieux/le mieux must not be confused with meilleur/le meilleur which are adjectives, used in front of a noun.

elle chante mieux que toi
she sings better than you (do)

c'est elle qui chante le mieux
she sings best

elle est meilleure chanteuse que toi
she is a better singer than you

c'est la meilleure chanteuse
she is the best singer

• Pis/le pis are only found in certain set expressions or in literary French:

tant pis
too bad

de mal en pis
from bad to worse

il n'y a rien de pis que cela
there is nothing worse than that

on en dit pis que pendre
nobody has a good word to say about it

6 PRONOUNS AND CORRESPONDING ADJECTIVES

A DEMONSTRATIVES

1 Demonstrative adjectives

a) **ce**

ce is often used to point out a particular person or thing, or persons or things. It is followed by the noun to which it refers and agrees in number and gender with that noun:

- ❏ with a masculine singular noun: **ce (cet)** this/that
- ❏ with a feminine singular noun: **cette** this/that
- ❏ with a plural noun (masc or fem): **ces** these/those

ce roman m'a beaucoup plu
I really liked this novel

il a neigé ce matin
it snowed this morning

cette chanson m'énerve
that song gets on my nerves

cette fois, c'est fini!
this time, it's over!

tu trouves que ces lunettes me vont bien?
do you think these glasses suit me?

cet is used instead of ce in front of a masculine singular word that begins with a vowel or a silent h:

cet été
this summer

cet hôtel
that hotel

b) **-ci** *and* **-là**

French does not have separate words to distinguish between 'this' and 'that'. However, when a particular emphasis is being placed on a person or object, or when a contrast is being made between persons or objects, -ci and -là are added to the noun:

-ci		this/these
	translates the idea of	
-là		that/those

je suis très occupé ces jours-ci
I'm very busy these days

que faisiez-vous ce soir-là?
what were you doing that evening?

tu préfères cette robe-ci ou cette robe-là?
do you prefer this dress or that dress?

2 Demonstrative pronouns

Demonstrative pronouns are used instead of a noun with ce/cette/ces. They are:

```
celui, celle, ceux, celles
ce
ceci, cela, ça
```

a) celui

celui agrees in number and gender with the noun it refers to. It has four different forms:

	MASCULINE	FEMININE
singular	celui	celle
plural	ceux	celles

PRONOUNS AND CORRESPONDING ADJECTIVES

celui, celle, ceux and celles cannot be used on their own. They are used:

i) with -ci or -là, for emphasis or for contrast:

celui-ci	celle-ci	this (one)
celui-là	celle-là	that (one)
ceux-ci	celles-ci	these (ones)
ceux-là	celles-là	those (ones)

j'aime bien ce maillot mais celui-là est moins cher
I like this swimsuit, but that one is cheaper

je voudrais ces fleurs – lesquelles? celles-ci ou celles-là?
I'd like these flowers – which ones? these or those?

ii) with de + noun, to express possession:

je préfère mon ordinateur à celui de Jean-Claude
I prefer my computer to Jean-Claude's

range ta chambre plutôt que celle de ta sœur
tidy your own bedroom rather than your sister's

mes parents sont moins sévères que ceux de Nicole
my parents aren't as strict as Nicole's

les douches municipales sont mieux que celles du camping
the public showers are better than those at the campsite

iii) with the relative pronouns qui, que, dont to introduce a relative clause (*for use of these relative pronouns, see pp 90-7*).

celui/celle/ceux/celles qui	the one(s) who/which
celui/celle/ceux/celles que	the one(s) whom/which
celui/celle/ceux/celles dont	the one(s) of which/whose

lequel est ton père? celui qui a une moustache?
which one is your father? the one with the moustache?

regarde cette voiture! celle qui est garée au coin
look at that car! the one which is parked at the corner

deux filles, celles qu'il avait rencontrées la veille
two girls, the ones he had met the day before

voilà mon copain, celui dont je t'ai parlé l'autre jour
here's my friend, the one I told you about the other day

PRONOUNS AND CORRESPONDING ADJECTIVES

b) ce

ce (meaning 'it' or 'that') is normally used with the verb être:

c'est	ce serait	c'était
it's/that's	it/that would be	it/that was

Note that ce changes to c' before an e or an é.

i) with a noun or pronoun, ce is used to identify people or things, or to emphasize them; it is translated in a variety of ways:

qu'est-ce que c'est? – c'est mon billet d'avion
what's that? – it's my plane ticket

qui est-ce? – c'est moi
who is it? – it's me

ce doit être lui
that must be him

c'est un artiste bien connu
he's a well-known artist

ce sont mes amis
they're my friends

ce sont des gens sympathiques
they're nice people

ce ne sont pas mes chaussures
those aren't my shoes

c'était une bonne idée
it was a good idea

c'est la dernière fois!
it's the last time!

c'est celui que j'ai vu
he's the one I saw

c'est elle qui l'a fait
she's the one who did it

ii) before an adjective, ce is used to refer to an idea, an event or a fact which has already been mentioned; it does not refer to any specific noun:

c'était formidable
it was great

ce serait amusant
it would be funny

oui, c'est vrai
yes, that's true

c'est sûr?
is that definite?

ce n'est pas grave
it doesn't matter/it's not serious

c'est bon à entendre
that's good to hear

c'est exact!
that's right!

c'est rare qu'il pleuve en juin
it doesn't often rain in June

Note that the translation of 'it' is an area of some difficulty for students of French, as it is sometimes translated by ce and sometimes by il/elle; see pp 251-3 for further information.

PRONOUNS AND CORRESPONDING ADJECTIVES

c) ceci, cela, ça

ceci (this), cela (that) and ça (that) are used to refer to an idea, an event, a fact or an object. They never refer to a particular noun already mentioned.

non, je n'aime pas ça!
no, I don't like that!

ça, c'est un acteur!
that's what I call an actor!

ça m'est égal
I don't mind

buvez ceci, ça vous fera du bien
drink this, it'll do you good

cela s'appelle comment, en anglais?
what do you call this in English?

ah, bon? cela m'étonne
really? that surprises me

souvenez-vous de ceci
remember this

cela ne vous regarde pas
that's none of your business

ça alors!
well, really!

Note that ceci is not very common in French; cela and ça are often used to translate 'this' as well as 'that'; ça is used far more frequently than cela in spoken French.

 B **INDEFINITE ADJECTIVES AND PRONOUNS**

1 Indefinite adjectives

They are:

MASCULINE	FEMININE	
autre(s)	autre(s)	other
certain(s)	certaine(s)	certain
chaque	chaque	each, every
même(s)	même(s)	same
plusieurs	plusieurs	several
quelque(s)	quelque(s)	some
tel(s)	telle(s)	such
tout (tous)	toute(s)	all, every

Note that, when used as indefinite adjectives, all the above adjectives are placed before the nouns to which they refer. Certain and même can be found after the noun but they will then have a different meaning (*see pp 44-6*).

a) chaque *and* plusieurs

chaque (each) is always singular, plusieurs (several) always plural; the feminine form is the same as the masculine form:

j'y vais chaque jour	**chaque personne**
I go there every day	each person
plusieurs années	**il a plusieurs amis**
several years	he's got several friends

b) autre, même *and* quelque

autre (other), même (same) and quelque (some) agree in number with the noun that follows; the feminine is the same as the masculine:

je voudrais un autre café	**d'autres couleurs**
I'd like another coffee	other colours
la même taille	**les mêmes touristes**
the same size	the same tourists
quelque temps après	**à quelques kilomètres**
some time later	a few kilometres away

c) certain, tel *and* tout

certain (certain, some), tel (such) and tout (all) agree in number and gender with the noun; they have four different forms:

un certain charme	**une certaine dame**
a certain charm	a certain lady
à certains moments	**certaines personnes**
at (certain) times	some people
un tel homme	**une telle aventure**
such a man	such an adventure

PRONOUNS AND CORRESPONDING ADJECTIVES

de tels avantages such advantages	**de telles difficultés** such difficulties

quoi! tu as mangé tout le fromage et tous les fruits?
what! you've eaten all the cheese and all the fruit?

toute la journée all day long	**toutes mes matières** all my subjects

Note

- Tel: the position of the article un/une with tel is not the same as in English: un tel homme = such a man.

- Tel cannot qualify another adjective; when it is used as an adverb, 'such' is translated by si or tellement:

  c'était un si bon repas/un repas tellement bon!
  it was such a good meal!

- Tous les/toutes les are often translated by 'every':

tous les jours every day	**toutes les places** all seats, every seat

2 Indefinite pronouns

a) These are:

MASCULINE	FEMININE	
aucun	aucune	none, not any
autre(s)	autre(s)	another one, other ones
certains	certaine(s)	certain, some
chacun	chacune	each one, every one, everyone,
on		one, someone, you, they, people, we
personne		nobody
plusieurs	plusieurs	several (ones)
quelque chose		something, anything
quelqu'un		someone
quelques-uns	quelques-unes	some, a few
rien		nothing
tout (tous)	toute(s)	everything, every one, all

PRONOUNS AND CORRESPONDING ADJECTIVES

pas celui-là, l'autre
not that one, the other one

certains disent que ...
some say that ...

qui est là? – personne
who's there? – nobody

plusieurs d'entre eux
several of them

il manque quelque chose?
is anything missing?

quelqu'un l'a averti
someone warned him

j'ai tout oublié
I've forgotten everything

elles sont toutes arrivées
they've all arrived

où sont les autres?
where are the others?

personne n'est venu
no one came

qu'as-tu? – rien
what's wrong? – nothing

chacun pour soi!
every man for himself!

dis quelque chose!
say something!

il y a quelqu'un?
is anyone in?

c'est tout, merci
that's all, thanks

allons-y tous ensemble
let's all go together

b) *Points to note*

i) aucun(e), personne and rien: these can be used on their own, but they are more often used with a verb and the negative word ne (*see* Negative Expressions, pp 239–42):

personne n'habite ici
no one lives here

il n'y a rien à manger
there's nothing to eat

ii) aucun(e), un(e) autre, d'autres, certain(e)s, plusieurs and quelques-un(e)s: when these pronouns are used as direct objects, the pronoun en must be used before the verb:

je n'en ai lu aucun
I haven't read any (of them)

donne-m'en une autre
give me another one

j'en ai vu d'autres qui étaient moins chers
I saw other ones which were cheaper

j'en connais certains
I know some of them

il y en a plusieurs
there are several

tu m'en donnes quelques-uns?
will you give me a few?

achètes-en quelques-unes
buy a few

    iii) **personne, quelque chose, rien, plusieurs**: when these are followed by an adjective, the preposition **de** (or **d'**) must be used in front of the adjective:

il n'y a personne de libre	**quelque chose de mieux**
there's no one available	something better
il y en avait plusieurs de cassés	**rien de grave**
several of them were broken	nothing serious

    iv) **autre** is commonly used in the following expressions:

quelqu'un d'autre	**quelque chose d'autre**	**rien d'autre**
someone else	something else	nothing else

c) **on**

This pronoun is used in a variety of ways in French. It can mean:

    i) *one/you/they/people* in a general sense:

on ne sait jamais	**on ne doit pas mentir**
you/one never know(s)	you shouldn't lie
en France, on roule à droite	
in France, they drive on the right	

    ii) *someone* (an undefined person)

In this sense, **on** is often translated by the passive (*see* p 156):

on me l'a déjà dit	**on vous l'apportera**
someone's already told me	someone will bring it to you
I've already been told	it will be brought to you

    iii) *we*

In spoken French, **on** is frequently used instead of **nous**; although it refers to a plural subject, it is followed by the third person singular:

qu'est-ce qu'on fait?	**fais vite, on t'attend!**
what shall we do?	hurry up, we're waiting for you!

Note that in compound tenses with the auxiliary être, the agreement of the past participle with on is optional:

on est allé au cinéma   **on est rentré en taxi**
on est allés au cinéma   **on est rentrées en taxi**
we went to the cinema   we went home by taxi

C INTERROGATIVE AND EXCLAMATORY ADJECTIVES AND PRONOUNS

1 The interrogative adjective quel?

a) *Forms*

quel (which, what) agrees in number and gender with the noun it refers to. It has four forms:

❏ with a masculine singular noun: quel?
❏ with a feminine singular noun: quelle?
❏ with a masculine plural noun: quels?
❏ with a feminine plural noun: quelles?

b) *Direct questions:*

quel est votre passe-temps favori?
what's your favourite pastime?

quelle heure est-il?   **quels jours as-tu de libres?**
what time is it?   which days have you got free?

quelles affaires comptes-tu prendre avec toi?
what/which things do you intend to take with you?

c) *Indirect questions:*

je ne sais pas quel CD choisir
I don't know which CD to choose

il se demande quelle veste lui va le mieux
he's wondering which jacket suits him best

2 The exclamatory adjective quel!

quel! has the same forms as the interrogative adjective quel?:

quel dommage!
what a pity!

quelle belle maison!
what a beautiful house!

quels imbéciles!
what idiots!

quelles jolies chaussures!
what lovely shoes!

3 Interrogative pronouns

These are:

lequel/laquelle/lesquels/lesquelles?	which (one(s))?
qui?	who?/whom?
que?	what?
quoi?	what?
ce qui	what
ce que	what

ce qui and ce que are used only in indirect questions; all other interrogative pronouns can be used both in direct and indirect questions.

a) lequel?

i) forms

lequel (which?, which one?) agrees in gender and in number with the noun it stands for:

❏ with a masculine singular noun:	lequel?	which (one)?
❏ with a feminine singular noun:	laquelle?	which (one)?
❏ with a masculine plural noun:	lesquels?	which (ones)?
❏ with a feminine plural noun:	lesquelles?	which (ones)?

After the prepositions à and de, the following changes occur:

à + lequel?	auquel?
à + lesquels?	auxquels?
à + lesquelles?	auxquelles?
de + lequel?	duquel?
de + lesquels?	desquels?
de + lesquelles?	desquelles?

Note that à/de + laquelle? do not contract.

ii) direct questions:

je cherche un hôtel; lequel recommandez-vous?
I'm looking for a hotel; which one do you recommend?

nous avons plusieurs couleurs; vous préférez laquelle?
we have several colours; which one do you prefer?

lesquels de ces livres sont à toi?
which of these books are yours?

je voudrais essayer ces chaussures – lesquelles?
I would like to try these shoes on – which ones?

iii) indirect questions:

demande-lui lequel de ces ordinateurs est le moins cher
ask him/her which (one) of these computers is the cheapest

c'est dans une de ces rues mais je ne sais plus laquelle
it's in one of these streets, but I can't remember which one

b) qui?

qui (who?, whom?) is used to refer to people; it can be both subject and object and can be used after a preposition:

qui t'a accompagné?
who came/went with you?

qui as-tu appelé?
who did you call?

tu y vas avec qui?
who are you going with?

c'est pour qui?
who is it for?

pour qui vous prenez-vous?
who do you think you are?

à qui l'as-tu donné?
who did you give it to?

Note that qui does **not** contract to qu' before a vowel or a silent h:

qui est-ce qu'elle attend?
who is she waiting for?

qui? can be replaced by qui est-ce qui? (subject) or qui est-ce que? (object) in direct questions:

qui est-ce qui veut du café?
who wants coffee?

qui est-ce que tu as vu?
who did you see?

avec qui est-ce que tu sors ce soir?
who are you going out with tonight?

Note, however, that qui cannot be replaced by qui est-ce qui or qui est-ce que in indirect questions:

j'aimerais savoir qui vous a dit ça
I'd like to know who told you that

elle se demandait de qui étaient les fleurs
she was wondering who the flowers were from

For more details on the use of qui/que *as relative pronouns, see pp 90–7.*

c) que?
que (what?) is used to refer to things. It is only used in direct questions, is always a direct object and cannot be used after prepositions:

que désirez-vous?
what would you like?

qu'a-t-il dit?
what did he say?

que? is rather formal and is usually replaced by qu'est-ce qui? or qu'est-ce que? in spoken French.

Note that que becomes qu' before a vowel or a silent h.

d) qu'est-ce qui?

qu'est-ce qui? (what?) is used as the subject of a verb; it cannot refer to a person:

qu'est-ce qui t'est arrivé?   **qu'est-ce qui la fait rire?**
what happened to you?   what makes her laugh?

e) qu'est-ce que?

qu'est-ce que? (what?) replaces que? as the object of a verb; it becomes qu'est-ce qu' before a vowel or a silent h:

qu'est-ce que tu aimes lire?
what do you like reading?

qu'est-ce qu'il va faire pendant les vacances?
what's he going to do during the holidays?

f) quoi?

quoi? (what?) refers to things; it is used:

i) instead of que or qu'est-ce que after a preposition:

à quoi penses-tu?   **dans quoi l'as-tu mis?**
what are you thinking about?   what did you put it in?

ii) in indirect questions:

demandez-lui de quoi il a besoin
ask him what he needs

je ne sais pas à quoi ça sert
I don't know what it's for

g) ce qui, ce que

ce qui and ce que (what) are only used in indirect questions; they replace qu'est-ce qui and (qu'est-ce) que.

They are used in the same way as the relative pronouns ce qui and ce que (*see* pp 95-6).

i) ce qui is used as the subject of the verb in the indirect question (ce qui is the subject of s'est passé in the following example):

nous ne saurons jamais ce qui s'est passé
we'll never know what happened

ii) ce que (ce qu' before a vowel or a silent h) is used as the object of the verb in the indirect question (ce que is the object of il faisait in the following example):

je n'ai pas remarqué ce qu'il faisait
I didn't notice what he was doing

 D PERSONAL PRONOUNS

There are four categories of personal pronouns:

subject pronouns
object pronouns
disjunctive pronouns
reflexive pronouns (*see* pp 115-7)

1 Subject pronouns

PERSON		SINGULAR	PLURAL	
1st	je (j')	I	nous	we
2nd	tu	you	vous	you
3rd	il	he, it	ils	they
	elle	she, it	elles	they
	on	one, we, they		

Note

• Je changes to j' before a vowel or a silent h:

j'ai honte   **j'adore les frites**
I'm ashamed   I love chips

j'habite en Écosse
I live in Scotland

Note—cont'd

- **Tu/vous**

  Vous can be plural or singular; it is used when speaking to more than one person (plural), or to a stranger or an older person (singular):

  vous venez, les gars?
  are you coming, guys?
  pourriez-vous m'indiquer la gare?
  could you show me the way to the station?

  Tu is used when speaking to a friend, a relative, a younger person, or someone else you know well:

  tu viens, Marc?
  are you coming, Marc?

- **Il/ils, elle/elles** may refer to people, animals or things, and must be of the same gender as the noun they replace:

ton stylo? il est là	**ta montre? elle est là**
your pen? there *it* is	your watch? there *it* is
tes gants? ils sont là	**tes lunettes? elles sont là**
your gloves? there *they* are	your glasses? there *they* are

  When referring to several nouns of different genders, French uses the masculine plural ils:

  j'ai trouvé dans mon sac un stylo et une montre. Ils ne m'appartiennent pas
  I found a pen and a watch in my bag. *They* don't belong to me

- *For information on* on, *see* pp 68-9.

2 Object pronouns

There are three types of object pronouns:

  direct object pronouns
  indirect object pronouns
  the pronouns en and y

PRONOUNS AND CORRESPONDING ADJECTIVES

a) *Forms*

	PERSON	DIRECT	INDIRECT
singular	1st	me (m') me	me (m') (to) me
	2nd	te (t') you	te (t') (to) you
	3rd	le (l') him, it	lui (to) him
		la (l') her, it	lui (to) her
plural	1st	nous us	nous (to) us
	2nd	vous you	vous (to) you
	3rd	les them	leur (to) them

Note

- Me, te, le and la change to m', t' and l' before a vowel or a silent h:

  il m'énerve!
  he gets on my nerves!

  je m'habituerai à lui
  I'll get used to him

- Te and vous: the same distinction should be made as between the subject pronouns tu and vous (*see* p 75).

- Le is sometimes used in an impersonal sense to refer to a fact, a statement or an idea which has already been expressed; it is usually not translated in English:

  elle a eu un bébé – je le sais, elle me l'a dit
  she's had a baby – I know, she told me

  j'irai aux États-Unis un jour; en tout cas je l'espère
  I'll go to the States one day; I hope so anyway

Note—cont'd

- When used as an indirect object pronoun, lui can be masculine or feminine:

pose-lui la question
ask him/her the question

j'ai décidé de lui offrir un cadeau
I've decided to give him/her a present

- When they are used with imperatives, moi and toi are used instead of me and te, except when en follows:

écris-moi bientôt
write to me soon

donne m'en
give me some

b) *Position*

In French, object pronouns come immediately before the verb they refer to. With a compound tense, they come before the auxiliary:

on t'attendra ici
we'll wait for you here

je l'ai rencontrée en ville
I met her in town

Note that when there are two verbs, the pronoun comes immediately before the verb to which it refers:

j'aimerais lui demander
I'd like to ask him/her

tu l'as entendu chanter?
have you heard him sing?

In positive commands (the affirmative imperative) the pronoun follows the verb and is joined to it by a hyphen:

regarde-les!
look at them!

parle-lui!
speak to him/her!

dis-nous ce qui s'est passé
tell us what happened

c) *Direct pronouns and indirect pronouns*

i) Direct object pronouns replace a noun which directly follows the verb. They answer the question 'who(m)?' or 'what?'

qui as-tu vu?	**j'ai vu mon ami; je l'ai vu**
who(m) did you see?	I saw *my friend*; I saw *him*
tu me connais	**j'aime le voir danser**
you know *me*	I like to see *him* dance
je les ai trouvés	**ne nous ennuie pas!**
I found *them*	don't bother *us*!

ii) Indirect object pronouns replace a noun which follows the verb with a linking preposition (usually à, to whom?). They answer the question 'who to?'

à qui as-tu parlé?	**j'ai parlé à Marc; je lui ai parlé**
who did you speak to?	I spoke *to Marc*; I spoke *to him*
elle lui a menti	**je te donne ce CD**
she lied *to him/her*	I'm giving this CD *to you*
je ne leur parle plus	
I'm not talking *to them* any more	

iii) le/la/les or lui/leur?

Direct pronouns differ from indirect pronouns only in the 3rd person and great care must be taken to use the correct one:

❑ English indirect object pronouns often look like direct objects; this becomes obvious when the object is placed at the end of the clause, after a linking preposition:

I showed him your photo
= I showed your photo to him
je lui ai montré ta photo

This is particularly the case with the following verbs:

acheter	to buy	**offrir**	to offer, to give
donner	to give	**prêter**	to lend
montrer	to show	**vendre**	to sell

je lui ai acheté un livre
I bought him/her a book
= I bought a book *for him/her*

ne leur prête pas mes affaires
don't lend them my things
= don't lend my things *to them*

❏ Some verbs take a direct object in English and an indirect object in French (*see* p 201):

je ne lui ai rien dit
I didn't tell *him/her* anything

je leur demanderai
I'll ask *them*

tu lui ressembles
you look like *him/her*

téléphone-leur
phone *them*

❏ Some verbs take a direct object in French and an indirect object in English (*see* p 200):

je l'attends
I'm waiting *for him/her*

écoutez-les!
listen *to them*!

d) *Order of object pronouns*
When several object pronouns are used together, they come in the following order:

i) Before the verb:

1	me	te		nous	vous
2		le	la	les	
3			lui	leur	

il me l'a donné
he gave it to me

je vais vous les envoyer
I'll send them to you

ne la leur vends pas
don't sell it to them

je le lui ai acheté
I bought it for him/her

ii) After the verb:

With a positive command (the affirmative imperative), the order is as follows:

1		le	la		les	
2	moi (m')	toi (t')		nous		vous
3		lui	leur			

apporte-les-moi!
bring them to me!

dites-le-lui!
tell him/her!

prête-la-nous!
lend it to us!

rends-la-leur!
give it back to them!

3 The pronoun en

a) *Use*

en is used instead of de + noun. Since de has a variety of meanings, en can be used in a number of ways:

i) It means 'of it/them', but also 'with it/them', 'about it/them', 'from it/there', 'out of it/there':

tu es sûr du prix? – j'en suis sûr
are you sure of the price? – I'm sure *of it*

je suis content de ce cadeau; j'en suis content
I'm pleased with this present; I'm pleased *with it*

elle est folle des animaux; elle en est folle
she's crazy about animals; she's crazy *about them*

il est descendu du train; il en est descendu
he got off the train; he got *off it*

il revient de Paris; il en revient
he's coming back from Paris; he's coming back *from there*

ii) Verbal constructions

Particular care should be taken with verbs and expressions which are followed by de + noun. Since de is not always translated in the same way, en may have a number of meanings:

il a envie de ce livre; il en a envie
he wants this book; he wants *it*

je te remercie de ton aide; je t'en remercie
thank you for your help; thank you *for it*

tu as besoin de ces papiers? tu en as besoin?
do you need these papers? do you need *them*?

elle a peur des chiens; elle en a peur
she's afraid of dogs; she's afraid *of them*

tu te souviens de ce film? tu t'en souviens?
do you remember this film? do you remember *it*?

iii) 'some'/'any'

en replaces the partitive article (du, de la, des) + noun; it means 'some'/'any':

tu veux du café? – non, je n'en veux pas
do you want (any) coffee? – no, I don't want *any*

j'achète des fruits? – non, j'en ai chez moi
shall I buy (some) fruit? – no, I've got *some* at home

il y a de la place? – en voilà là-bas
is there any room? – there's some over there

iv) Expressions of quantity

en must be used with expressions of quantity not followed by a noun. It replaces de + noun and means 'of it/them', but is seldom translated in English:

tu as pris assez d'argent? tu en as pris assez?
did you take enough money? did you take enough?

vous avez combien de frères? – j'en ai deux
how many brothers do you have? – I've got two

j'ai fini mes cigarettes; je vais en acheter un paquet
I've finished my cigarettes; I'm going to buy a packet

b) *Position*

Like object pronouns, en comes immediately before the verb, except with positive commands (the affirmative imperative), where it comes after the verb and is linked to it by a hyphen:

j'en veux un kilo	**j'en ai marre!**
I want a kilo (of it/them)	I'm fed up (with it)!
prends-en assez?	**laisses-en aux autres!**
take enough (of it/them)!	leave some for the others!

When used in conjunction with other object pronouns, it always comes last:

ne m'en parlez pas!	**je vous en donnerai**
don't tell me about it!	I'll give you some
prête-lui-en!	**gardez-nous-en!**
lend him/her some!	keep some for us!

4 The pronoun y

a) *Use*

y is used instead of à + noun, but never refers to a person. It is used:

i) As the indirect object of a verb. Since the preposition à is translated in a variety of ways in English, y may have various meanings (it, of it/them, about it/them *etc*):

tu joues au tennis? – non, j'y joue rarement
do you play tennis? – no, I seldom play (*it*)

je pense à mon pays natal; j'y pense souvent
I'm thinking *about* my home country; I often think *about it*

il s'intéresse à la photo; il s'y intéresse
he's interested in photography; he's interested *in it*

ii) To mean 'there':

j'ai passé deux jours à Londres; j'y ai passé deux jours
I spent two days in London; I spent two days there

il est allé en Grèce; il y est allé
he went to Greece; he went there

Note that y must always be used with the verb aller (to go)
when the place is not mentioned in the clause. It is often not
translated in English:

comment vas-tu à l'école? – j'y vais en bus
how do you get to school? – I go (there) by bus

allons-y!
let's go!
(lit. 'let's go there!')

on y va demain
we're going (there) tomorrow

iii) To replace the prepositions en, dans, sur + noun; y then means
'there', 'in it/them', 'on it/them':

je voudrais vivre en France; je voudrais y vivre
I'd like to live in France; I'd like to live *there*

je les ai mis dans ma poche; je les y ai mis
I put them in my pocket; I put them *there*

sur la table? □ non, je ne l'y vois pas
on the table? no, I don't see it *there*

b) *Position*

Like other object pronouns, y comes immediately before the verb,
except with a positive command (the affirmative imperative),
where it must follow the verb:

j'y réfléchirai
I'll think about it

il s'y est habitué
he got used to it

pensez-y!
think about it!

n'y allez pas!
don't go (there)!

When used with other object pronouns, y comes last:

il va nous y rencontrer
he'll meet us there

je l'y ai vu hier
I saw him there yesterday

5 Disjunctive pronouns

a) *Forms*

PERSON	SINGULAR	PLURAL
1st	moi	nous
	me	us
2nd	toi	vous
	you	you
3rd (masculine)	lui	eux
	him	them
(feminine)	elle	elles
	her	them
(impersonal)	soi	
	oneself	

Note

• Toi/vous: the same difference should be made as between tu and vous (*see* p 75).

• Soi is used in an impersonal, general sense to refer to indefinite pronouns and adjectives (on, chacun, tout le monde, personne, chaque *etc*); it is mainly found in set phrases, such as:

chacun pour soi   **cela va de soi**
every man for himself   that goes without saying

b) *Use*

Disjunctive pronouns, also called emphatic pronouns, are used instead of object pronouns when referring to persons in the following cases:

i) In answer to a question, alone or in a phrase without a verb:

qui est là? – moi
who's there? – me

j'ai aimé ce film; et toi?
I liked that film; did you?

qui préfères-tu, lui ou elle? – elle, bien sûr
who do you prefer, him or her? – her, of course

ii) After c'est/ce sont, c'était/c'étaient *etc*:

ouvrez, c'est moi!
open up, it's me!

non, ce n'était pas lui
no, it wasn't him

iii) After a preposition:

vous allez chez lui?
are you going to his place?

tu y vas avec elle?
are you going with her?

regarde devant toi!
look in front of you!

oh, c'est pour moi?
oh, is that for me?

iv) With verbal constructions. Special care should be taken when the verb is followed by a preposition:

tu peux compter sur moi
you can count on me

quoi! tu as peur de lui?
what! you're afraid of him?

il m'a parlé de toi
he told me about you

je pense souvent à vous
I often think about you

Note that emphatic pronouns are only used when referring to people. In other cases y or en must be used.

v) For emphasis, particularly when two pronouns are contrasted. The unstressed subject pronoun is usually included:

vous, vous m'énervez!
you get on my nerves!

lui, il joue bien; elle, non
he plays well; *she* doesn't

moi, je n'aime pas l'hiver
I don't like winter

eux, ils sont partis
they've left

vi) In the case of multiple subjects (two pronouns or one pronoun and one noun):

lui et son frère sont dans l'équipe
he and his brother are in the team

ma famille et moi allons très bien
my family and I are very well

vii) As the second element of a comparison:

il est plus sympa que toi
he is nicer than you

elle chante mieux que lui
she sings better than he does

viii) Before a relative pronoun:

c'est lui que j'aime
he's the one I love

c'est toi qui l'as dit
you're the one who said it

lui qui n'aime pas le vin blanc en a bu quatre verres
he who doesn't like white wine had four glasses

ix) With -même(s) (-self, -selves), aussi (too), seul (alone):

faites-le vous-mêmes
do it yourselves

j'irai moi-même
I'll go myself

lui aussi est parti
he too went away

elle seule le sait
she alone knows

x) To replace a possessive pronoun (*see* pp 89–90):

c'est le mien; il est à moi
it's mine; it belongs to me

cette valise n'est pas à lui?
doesn't that suitcase belong to him?

 E POSSESSIVE ADJECTIVES AND PRONOUNS

1 Possessive adjectives

a) *Forms*

Possessive adjectives always come before their related noun. Like other adjectives, they agree in gender and number

PRONOUNS AND CORRESPONDING ADJECTIVES

with the noun; the masculine and feminine plural forms are
identical:

SINGULAR MASCULINE	FEMININE	PLURAL (MASC AND FEM)	
mon	ma	mes	my
ton	ta	tes	your
son	sa	ses	his/her/its/one's
notre	notre	nos	our
votre	votre	vos	your
leur	leur	leurs	their

j'ai mis mon argent et mes affaires dans mon sac
I've put my money and my things in my bag

comment va ton frère? et ta sœur? et tes parents?
how's your brother? and your sister? and your parents?

notre rue est assez calme   **ce sont vos amis**
our street is fairly quiet   they're your friends

Note that mon/ton/son are used instead of ma/ta/sa when the next
word starts with a vowel or silent h:

mon ancienne maison   **ton amie Christine**
my old house   your friend Christine

son haleine sentait l'alcool
his/her breath smelled of alcohol

b) *Use*

   i) The possessive adjective is repeated before each noun and
      agrees in number and gender with it:
      mon père et ma mère sont sortis
      my mother and father have gone out

   ii) son/sa/ses
       son, sa and ses can all mean 'his', 'her' or 'its'. In French,
       the form of the adjective is determined by the gender

and number of the noun that follows, and not by the possessor:

il m'a prêté sa mobylette et son casque
he lent me his moped and his helmet

elle s'entend bien avec sa mère mais pas avec son père
she gets on well with her mother, but not with her father

elle vit pour son travail; lui pour ses enfants
she lives for her job; he lives for his children

iii) ton/ta/tes and votre/vos

The two sets of words for 'your', ton/ta/tes and votre/vos, correspond to the two different forms of tu and vous; they must not be used together with the same person:

tu as parlé à ton patron?
have you spoken to your boss?

Monsieur, vous oubliez votre parapluie!
excuse me, sir, you've forgotten your umbrella!

iv) In French, the possessive adjective is replaced by the definite article (le/la/les) with the following:

❏ parts of the body:

il s'est essuyé les mains	**elle a haussé les épaules**
he wiped his hands	she shrugged (her shoulders)

❏ descriptive phrases at the end of a clause, where English adds 'with':

il marchait lentement, les mains dans les poches
he was walking slowly, with his hands in his pockets

elle l'a regardé partir, les larmes aux yeux
she watched him leave with tears in her eyes

2 Possessive pronouns

SINGULAR		PLURAL	
MASCUINE	**FEMININE**	**(MASC AND FEM)**	
le mien	la mienne	les mien(ne)s	mine
le tien	la tienne	les tien(ne)s	yours
le sien	la sienne	les sien(ne)s	his/hers/its
le nôtre	la nôtre	les nôtres	ours
le vôtre	la vôtre	les vôtres	yours
le leur	la leur	les leurs	theirs

Possessive pronouns are used instead of a possessive adjective + noun. They agree in gender and in number with the noun they stand for, and not with the possessor (it is particularly important to remember this when translating 'his' and 'hers'):

j'aime bien ton appartement mais je préfère le mien
I quite like your flat, but I prefer mine

on prend quelle voiture? la mienne ou la tienne?
which car shall we take? mine or yours?

comment sont vos profs? les nôtres sont sympas
what are your teachers like? ours are nice

j'avais mon passeport mais Brigitte avait oublié le sien
I had my passport, but Brigitte had forgotten hers

j'ai gardé ma moto mais Paul a vendu la sienne
I've kept my motorbike but Paul has sold his

à or de + possessive pronoun

The prepositions à and de combine with the articles le and les in the usual way:

à + le mien	au mien
à + les miens	aux miens
à + les miennes	aux miennes
de + le mien	du mien
de + les miens	des miens
de + les miennes	des miennes

demande à tes parents, j'ai déjà parlé aux miens
ask your parents, I've already spoken to mine

leur appartement ressemble beaucoup au nôtre
their flat is very similar to ours

j'aime bien les chiens mais j'ai peur du tien
I like dogs, but I'm afraid of yours

Note that after the verb être, the possessive pronoun is often replaced by à + emphatic pronoun (*see* p 86):

à qui est cette écharpe? – elle est à moi
whose scarf is this? – it's mine

ce livre est à toi? – non, il est à elle
is this book yours? – no, it's hers

c'est à qui? à vous ou à lui?
whose is this? yours or his?

 F RELATIVE PRONOUNS

1 Definition

Relative pronouns are words which introduce a relative clause. In the sentence:

I bought the book which you recommended

'which' is the relative pronoun, 'which you recommended' is the relative clause and 'the book' is the antecedent (ie the noun to which the relative pronoun refers).

2 Forms

Relative pronouns are:

qui	who/which	lequel	which
que	who(m)/which	dont	of which/whose
quoi	what	ce qui	what
où	where	ce que	what

qui, que, quoi, lequel, ce qui and ce que can also be used as interrogative pronouns (*see* pp 70-4) and must not be confused with them.

3 Use

a) qui

qui is used as the subject of a relative clause. It means:

i) 'who', 'that' (referring to people):

est-ce que tu connais le monsieur qui habite ici?
do you know the man who lives here?

ce n'est pas lui qui a menti
he's not the one who lied

ii) 'which', 'that' (referring to things):

tu as pris le journal qui était sur la télé?
did you take the paper which/that was on the TV?

b) que

que (which contracts to qu' before a vowel or a silent h) is used as the object of a relative clause; it is often not translated. It means:

i) 'who(m)', 'that' (referring to people):

la fille que j'aime ne m'aime pas
the girl (that) I love doesn't love me

ii) 'which', 'that' (referring to things):

j'ai perdu le briquet qu'il m'a offert
I've lost the lighter (which/that) he gave me

c) qui *or* que?

qui (subject) and que (object) are translated by the same words in English (who, which, that). To use the correct pronoun in French, it is essential to know whether a relative pronoun is the object or the subject of the relative clause:

i) when the verb of the relative clause has its own subject, the object pronoun que must be used:

c'est un passe-temps que j'adore
it's a pastime (that) I love *(the subject of 'adore' is 'je')*

ii) otherwise the relative pronoun is the subject of the verb in the relative clause and the subject pronoun qui must be used:

j'ai trouvé un manteau qui me plaît
I've found a coat that I like *(the subject of 'plaît' is 'qui')*

d) lequel

i) forms

lequel (which) has four different forms, as it must agree with the noun to which it refers:

	SINGULAR	PLURAL	
masculine	lequel	lesquels	which
feminine	laquelle	lesquelles	

lequel *etc* combines with the prepositions à and de as follows:

à + lequel	auquel
à + lesquels	auxquels
à + lesquelles	auxquelles
de + lequel	duquel
de + lesquels	desquels
de + lesquelles	desquelles

à + laquelle and de + laquelle do not change.

quels sont les sports auxquels tu t'intéresses?
what sports are you interested *in*?

voilà le village près duquel on campait
here's the village which we camped near

ii) qui or lequel with a preposition?

When a relative pronoun follows a preposition, the pronoun used is either qui or lequel. In English, the relative pronoun is seldom used and the preposition is frequently placed after the verb or at the end of the sentence.

qui is generally used after a preposition when referring to people:

où est la fille avec qui je dansais?
where's the girl I was dancing *with*?

montre-moi la personnne à qui tu as vendu ton vélo
show me the person you sold your bike *to*

lequel is often used after a preposition when referring to things:

l'immeuble dans lequel j'habite est très moderne
the building (which) I live *in* is very modern

je ne reconnais pas la voiture avec laquelle il est venu
I don't recognize the car (which) he came *in*

lequel is also used when referring to persons after the prepositions entre (between) and parmi (among):

elle observait les invités parmi lesquels elle ne reconnaissait personne
she was watching the guests, none of whom she recognized

il y avait deux candidats, entre lesquels nous avons dû choisir
there were two candidates, between whom we had to choose

e) dont

dont is frequently used instead of de qui, duquel *etc.* It means:

i) 'of which'/'of whom':

un métier dont il est fier
a job (which) he is proud of

Care must be taken with verbs that are normally followed by de + object: de is not always translated by 'of' in English, and is sometimes not translated at all (*see section on verbal constructions pp 201–2*):

voilà les choses dont j'ai besoin
here are the things (*which*) I need

les gens dont tu parles ne m'intéressent pas
I'm not interested in the people you're talking about

l'enfant dont elle s'occupe n'est pas le sien
the child she is looking *after* is not hers

ii) 'whose'
dont is also used to translate the English pronoun 'whose'. In French, the construction of the clause that follows dont differs from English in two ways:

❏ the noun which follows dont is used with the definite article (le, la, les, l'):

mon copain, dont le père a eu un accident
my friend, whose father had an accident

❏ the word order in French is dont + subject + verb + object:

je te présente Hélène, dont tu connais déjà le frère
this is Hélène, whose brother you already know

c'était dans une petite rue dont j'ai oublié le nom
it was in a small street the name of which I've forgotten

Note that dont cannot be used after a preposition:

une jolie maison, près de laquelle il y a un petit lac
a pretty house, *next* to which there is a small lake

f) où

i) où generally means 'where':
l'hôtel où on a logé était très confortable
the hotel where we stayed was very confortable

ii) où often replaces a preposition + lequel, and means 'in/to/on/at which' *etc*:

c'est la maison où je suis né
that's the house in which/where I was born

une soirée où il a invité tous ses amis
a party to which he invited all his friends

iii) où is also used to translate 'when' after a noun referring to time:

le jour où	**la fois où**	**le moment où**
the day when	the time when	the moment when

tu te rappelles le soir où on a raté le dernier métro?
do you remember the evening when we missed the last train?

le jour où j'ai eu mon permis de conduire
the day when I got my driving licence

g) ce qui, ce que

ce is used before qui and que when the relative pronoun does not refer to a specific noun. Both ce qui and ce que mean 'that which', 'the thing which', and are usually translated by 'what':

i) ce qui

ce qui is followed by a verb without a subject (qui is the subject):

ce qui s'est passé ne vous regarde pas
what happened is none of your business

ce qui m'étonne, c'est sa patience
what surprises me is his patience

Note that in French, this structure requires a comma between the two clauses, and the second clause must be introduced by c'est/c'était/ce sera depending on the tense being used.

ii) ce que

ce que (ce qu' before a vowel or a silent h) is followed by a verb with its own subject (que is the object):

fais ce que tu veux
do what you want

c'est ce qu'il a dit?
is that what he said?

ce que vous me demandez est impossible
what you're asking me is impossible

iii) tout ce qui/que

tout is used in front of ce qui/que in the sense of 'all that', 'everything that':

c'est tout ce que je veux
that's all I want

tout ce que tu as fait
everything you did

tu n'as pas eu de mal; c'est tout ce qui compte
you weren't hurt; that's all that matters

iv) ce qui/que are often used in indirect questions (*see* pp 73-4):

je ne sais pas ce qu'ils vont dire
I don't know what they'll say

v) when referring to a previous clause, ce qui and ce que are translated by 'which':

elle est en retard, ce qui arrive souvent
she's late, which happens often

vi) ce qui/que are used with a preposition; ce qui is used as the subject of the verb in the relative clause and ce que is used as the object of the verb in the relative clause:

ce n'est pas étonnant, après ce qui nous est arrivé
it's not surprising, after what happened to us

il y a du vrai dans ce que vous dites
there is some truth in what you say

When a preposition is required by the verb in the relative clause, eg penser à, s'expliquer sur, quoi is used instead of ce que and comes after the preposition:

c'est ce à quoi je pensais
that's what I was thinking about

voici ce sur quoi il devra s'expliquer
this is what he'll have to explain

ce dont is used instead of de + ce que when de is the preposition required by the verb in the relative clause, eg avoir peur de, avoir besoin de:

c'est ce dont j'avais peur
that's what I was afraid of

tu as trouvé ce dont tu avais besoin?
did you find what you needed?

7 VERBS

A REGULAR CONJUGATIONS

1 Conjugations

There are three main conjugations in French, which are determined by the infinitive endings. The first conjugation verbs, by far the largest category, end in -er, eg aimer and will be referred to as **-er verbs**; the second conjugation verbs end in -ir, eg finir and will be referred to as **-ir verbs**; the third conjugation verbs, the smallest category, end in -re, eg vendre and will be referred to as **-re verbs**.

2 Simple tenses

The simple tenses in French are:

    present
    imperfect
    future
    conditional
    past historic
    present subjunctive
    imperfect subjunctive

For the use of the different tenses, *see* pp 122-30.

3 Formation of tenses

The tenses are formed by adding the following endings to the stem of the verb (usually the stem of the infinitive) as set out in the following section:

a) *PRESENT*: stem of the infinitive + the following endings:

-ER verbs	-IR verbs	-RE verbs
-e, -es, -e,	-is, -is, -it,	-s, -s, ø,
-ons, -ez, -ent	-issons, -issez, -issent	-ons, -ez, -ent
AIMER	FINIR	VENDRE
j'aime	je finis	je vends
tu aimes	tu finis	tu vends
il aime	il finit	il vend
elle aime	elle finit	elle vend
nous aimons	nous finissons	nous vendons
vous aimez	vous finissez	vous vendez
ils aiment	ils finissent	ils vendent
elles aiment	elles finissent	elles vendent

b) *IMPERFECT*: stem of the first person plural of the present indicative (ie the nous form minus -ons) + the following endings:

-ais, -ais, -ait, -ions, -iez, -aient

j'aimais	je finissais	je vendais
tu aimais	tu finissais	tu vendais
il/elle aimait	il/elle finissait	il/elle vendait
nous aimions	nous finissions	nous vendions
vous aimiez	vous finissiez	vous vendiez
ils/elles aimaient	ils/elles finissaient	ils/elles vendaient

Note that the only irregular imperfect is être: j'étais *etc*.

c) *FUTURE*: infinitive + the following endings:

-ai, -as, -a, -ons, -ez, -ont

Note that verbs ending in -re drop the final e of the infinitive.

j'aimerai	je finirai	je vendrai
tu aimeras	tu finiras	tu vendras
il/elle aimera	il/elle finira	il/elle vendra
nous aimerons	nous finirons	nous vendrons
vous aimerez	vous finirez	vous vendrez
ils/elles aimeront	ils/elles finiront	ils/elles vendront

d) *CONDITIONAL*: infinitive + the following endings:

-ais, -ais, -ait, -ions, -iez, -aient

Note that verbs ending in -re drop the final e of the infinitive.

j'aimerais	je finirais	je vendrais
tu aimerais	tu finirais	tu vendrais
il/elle aimerait	il/elle finirait	il/elle vendrait
nous aimerions	nous finirions	nous vendrions
vous aimeriez	vous finiriez	vous vendriez
ils/elles aimeraient	ils/elles finiraient	ils/elles vendraient

e) *PAST HISTORIC*: stem of the infinitive + the following endings:

-ER verbs	-IR verbs	-RE verbs
-ai, -as, -a,	-is, -is, -it,	-is, -is, -it,
-âmes, -âtes, -èrent	-îmes, -îtes, -irent	-îmes, -îtes, -irent
j'aimai	je finis	je vendis
tu aimas	tu finis	tu vendis
il/elle aima	il/elle finit	il/elle vendit
nous aimâmes	nous finîmes	nous vendîmes
vous aimâtes	vous finîtes	vous vendîtes
ils/elles aimèrent	ils/elles finirent	ils/elles vendirent

f) *PRESENT SUBJUNCTIVE*: stem of the first person plural of the present indicative (ie the nous form minus -ons) + the following endings:

-e, -es, -e, -ions, -iez, -ent

j'aime	je finisse	je vende
tu aimes	tu finisses	tu vendes
il/elle aime	il/elle finisse	il/elle vende
nous aimions	nous finissions	nous vendions
vous aimiez	vous finissiez	vous vendiez
ils/elles aiment	ils/elles finissent	ils/elles vendent

g) *IMPERFECT SUBJUNCTIVE*: stem of the first person singular of the past historic + the following endings:

-ER verbs	-IR verbs	-RE verbs
-asse, -asses, -ât, -assions, -assiez, -assent	-isse, -isses, -ît, -issions, -issiez, -issent	-isse, -isses, -ît, -issions, -issiez, -issent
j'aimasse	je finisse	je vendisse
tu aimasses	tu finisses	tu vendisses
il/elle aimât	il/elle finît	il/elle vendît
nous aimassions	nous finissions	nous vendissions
vous aimassiez	vous finissiez	vous vendissiez
ils/elles aimassent	ils/elles finissent	ils/elles vendissent

B STANDARD SPELLING IRREGULARITIES

Spelling irregularities only affect -er verbs.

1 Verbs ending in -cer and -ger

a) Verbs ending in -cer require a cedilla under the c (ç) before an a or an o to preserve the soft sound of the c: eg commencer (to begin); il commença (he began).

b) Verbs ending in -ger require an -e after the g before an a or an o to preserve the soft sound of the g: eg manger (to eat); je mangeais (I was eating).

Changes to -cer and -ger verbs occur in the following tenses: present, imperfect, past historic, imperfect subjunctive and present participle.

COMMENCER	MANGER
PRESENT	
je commence	je mange
tu commences	tu manges
il commence	il mange
elle commence	elle mange
nous commençons	nous mangeons
vous commencez	vous mangez
ils commencent	ils mangent
elles commencent	elles mangent
IMPERFECT	
je commençais	je mangeais
tu commençais	tu mangeais
il commençait	il mangeait
elle commençait	elle mangeait
nous commencions	nous mangions
vous commenciez	vous mangiez
ils commençaient	ils mangeaient
elles commençaient	elles mangeaient
PAST HISTORIC	
je commençai	je mangeai
tu commenças	tu mangeas
il commença	il mangea
elle commença	elle mangea
nous commençâmes	nous mangeâmes
vous commençâtes	vous mangeâtes
ils commencèrent	ils mangèrent
elles commencèrent	elles mangèrent

IMPERFECT SUBJUNCTIVE

je commençasse	je mangeasse
tu commençasses	tu mangeasses
il commençât	il mangeât
elle commençât	elle mangeât
nous commençassions	nous mangeassions
vous commençassiez	vous mangeassiez
ils commençassent	ils mangeassent
elles commençassent	elles mangeassent

PRESENT PARTICIPLE

commençant	mangeant

2 Verbs with other -er endings

a) Verbs ending in -eler

Verbs ending in -eler double the l before a silent e (ie before -e, -es, -ent of the present indicative and subjunctive, and throughout the future and present conditional): eg appeler (to call).

PRESENT INDICATIVE	PRESENT SUBJUNCTIVE
j'appelle	j'appelle
tu appelles	tu appelles
il appelle	il appelle
elle appelle	elle appelle
nous appelons	nous appelions
vous appelez	vous appeliez
ils appellent	ils appellent
elles appellent	elles appellent
FUTURE	**CONDITIONAL**
j'appellerai	j'appellerais
tu appelleras	tu appellerais
il appellera	il appellerait
elle appellera	elle appellerait
nous appellerons	nous appellerions
vous appellerez	vous appelleriez
ils appelleront	ils appelleraient
elles appelleront	elles appelleraient

Note, however, that some verbs ending in -eler, including the following, are conjugated like acheter (*see* p 106):

celer	to conceal
congeler	to (deep-) freeze
déceler	to detect, to reveal
dégeler	to defrost
geler	to freeze
harceler	to harass
marteler	to hammer
modeler	to model
peler	to peel

b) Verbs ending in -eter
Verbs ending in -eter double the t before a silent e (ie before -e, -es, -ent of the present indicative and subjunctive, and throughout the future and conditional): eg jeter (to throw).

PRESENT INDICATIVE	*PRESENT SUBJUNCTIVE*
je jette	je jette
tu jettes	tu jettes
il jette	il jette
elle jette	elle jette
nous jetons	nous jetions
vous jetez	vous jetiez
ils jettent	ils jettent
elles jettent	elles jettent
FUTURE	*CONDITIONAL*
je jetterai	je jetterais
tu jetteras	tu jetterais
il jettera	il jetterait
elle jettera	elle jetterait
nous jetterons	nous jetterions
vous jetterez	vous jetteriez
ils jetteront	ils jetteraient
elles jetteront	elles jetteraient

Note, however, that some verbs ending in -eter, including the following, are conjugated like acheter (*see* p 106):

crocheter	to pick *(a lock)*
fureter	to ferret about
haleter	to pant
racheter	to buy back

c) Verbs ending in -oyer and -uyer

In verbs ending in -oyer and -uyer the y changes to i before a silent e (ie before -e, -es, -ent of the present indicative and subjunctive, and throughout the future and conditional): eg employer (to use) and ennuyer (to bore).

PRESENT INDICATIVE	PRESENT SUBJUNCTIVE
j'emploie	j'emploie
tu emploies	tu emploies
il emploie	il emploie
elle emploie	elle emploie
nous employons	nous employions
vous employez	vous employiez
ils emploient	ils emploient
elles emploient	elles emploient

FUTURE	CONDITIONAL
j'emploierai	j'emploierais
tu emploieras	tu emploierais
il emploiera	il emploierait
elle emploiera	elle emploierait
nous emploierons	nous emploierions
vous emploierez	vous emploieriez
ils emploieront	ils emploieraient
elles emploieront	elles emploieraient

Note that envoyer (to send) and renvoyer (to dismiss) have an irregular future and conditional: j'enverrai, j'enverrais; je renverrai, je renverrais.

d) Verbs ending in -ayer

In verbs ending in -ayer, eg balayer (to sweep), payer (to pay), essayer (to try), the change from y to i is optional:

eg   je balaie/je balaye
                     je paie/je paye
                     j'essaie/j'essaye

e) Verbs ending in e- + consonant + -er

Verbs like acheter, enlever, mener, peser change the (last) e of the stem to è before a silent e (ie before -e, -es, -ent of the present indicative and subjunctive and throughout the future and conditional):

PRESENT INDICATIVE	PRESENT SUBJUNCTIVE
j'achète	j'achète
tu achètes	tu achètes
il achète	il achète
elle achète	elle achète
nous achetons	nous achetions
vous achetez	vous achetiez
ils achètent	ils achètent
elles achètent	elles achètent
FUTURE	*CONDITIONAL*
j'achèterai	j'achèterais
tu achèteras	tu achèterais
il achètera	il achèterait
elle achètera	elle achèterait
nous achèterons	nous achèterions
vous achèterez	vous achèteriez
ils achèteront	ils achèteraient
elles achèteront	elles achèteraient

Verbs conjugated like acheter include:

achever to complete	**haleter** to pant
amener to bring	**harceler** to harass
celer to conceal	**lever** to lift
crever to burst	**marteler** to hammer
crocheter to pick *(lock)*	**mener** to lead
élever to raise	**modeler** to model
emmener to take away	**peler** to peel
enlever to remove	**peser** to weigh
étiqueter to label	**se promener** to go for a walk
fureter to ferret about	**semer** to sow
geler to freeze	**soulever** to lift

f) Verbs ending in é- + consonant + -er

Verbs like espérer (to hope) change é to è before a silent e in the present indicative and subjunctive. Note, however, that in the future and conditional é is retained.

PRESENT INDICATIVE	PRESENT SUBJUNCTIVE
j'espère	j'espère
tu espères	tu espères
il espère	il espère
elle espère	elle espère
nous espérons	nous espérions
vous espérez	vous espériez
ils espèrent	ils espèrent
elles espèrent	elles espèrent
FUTURE	CONDITIONAL
j'espérerai	j'espérerais
tu espéreras	tu espérerais
il espérera	il espérerait
elle espérera	elle espérerait
nous espérerons	nous espérerions
vous espérerez	vous espéreriez
ils espéreront	ils espéreraient
elles espéreront	elles espéreraient

Verbs conjugated like espérer include verbs ending in -éder, -érer, -éter *etc*:

accéder	to accede to
céder	to yield
célébrer	to celebrate
compléter	to complete
considérer	to consider
décéder	to die
digérer	to digest
gérer	to manage
inquiéter	to worry
libérer	to free
opérer	to operate
pénétrer	to penetrate
persévérer	to persevere
posséder	to possess
précéder	to precede
préférer	to prefer
protéger	to protect
récupérer	to recover
refréner	to curb
régler	to rule
régner	to reign
répéter	to repeat, to rehearse
révéler	to reveal
sécher	to dry
succéder	to succeed
suggérer	to suggest
tolérer	to tolerate

C AUXILIARIES AND THE FORMATION OF COMPOUND TENSES

1 Formation

a) The two auxiliary verbs avoir and être are used with the past participle of a verb to form compound tenses.

b) *The past participle*

The regular past participle is formed by taking the stem of the infinitive and adding the following endings:

-ER verbs	-IR verbs	-RE verbs
aim(er) + é	fin(ir) + i	vend(re) + u
aimé	fini	vendu

For the agreement of past participles see **pp 154-6**.

c) *Compound tenses*

In French there are seven compound tenses: perfect, pluperfect, future perfect, past conditional (conditional perfect), past anterior, perfect subjunctive, pluperfect subjunctive.

2 Verbs conjugated with avoir

PERFECT	*PLUPERFECT*
present of avoir + past participle	imperfect of avoir + past participle
j'ai aimé	j'avais aimé
tu as aimé	tu avais aimé
il a aimé	il avait aimé
elle a aimé	elle avait aimé
nous avons aimé	nous avions aimé
vous avez aimé	vous aviez aimé
ils ont aimé	ils avaient aimé
elles ont aimé	elles avaient aimé

FUTURE PERFECT
future of **avoir** + past participle

j'aurai aimé
tu auras aimé
il aura aimé
elle aura aimé
nous aurons aimé
vous aurez aimé
ils auront aimé
elles auront aimé

PAST ANTERIOR
past historic of **avoir** + past participle

j'eus aimé
tu eus aimé
il eut aimé
elle eut aimé
nous eûmes aimé
vous eûtes aimé
ils eurent aimé
elles eurent aimé

PERFECT SUBJUNCTIVE
present subjunctive of **avoir** +
  past participle

j'aie aimé
tu aies aimé
il ait aimé
elle ait aimé
nous ayons aimé
vous ayez aimé
ils aient aimé
elles aient aimé

PAST CONDITIONAL
conditional of **avoir** + past participle

j'aurais aimé
tu aurais aimé
il aurait aimé
elle aurait aimé
nous aurions aimé
vous auriez aimé
ils auraient aimé
elles auraient aimé

PLUPERFECT SUBJUNCTIVE
imperfect subjunctive of **avoir** +
  past participle

j'eusse aimé
tu eusses aimé
il eût aimé
elle eût aimé
nous eussions aimé
vous eussiez aimé
ils eussent aimé
elles eussent aimé

3 Verbs conjugated with être

PERFECT
present of être + past participle

je suis arrivé(e)
tu es arrivé(e)
il est arrivé
elle est arrivée
nous sommes arrivé(e)s
vous êtes arrivé(e)(s)
ils sont arrivés
elles sont arrivées

FUTURE PERFECT
future of être + past participle

je serai arrivé(e)
tu seras arrivé(e)
il sera arrivé
elle sera arrivée
nous serons arrivé(e)s
vous serez arrivé(e)(s)
ils seront arrivés
elles seront arrivées

PAST ANTERIOR
past historic of être + past participle

je fus arrivé(e)
tu fus arrivé(e)
il fut arrivé
elle fut arrivée
nous fûmes arrivé(e)s
vous fûtes arrivé(e)(s)
ils furent arrivés
elles furent arrivées

PLUPERFECT
imperfect of être + past participle

j'étais arrivé(e)
tu étais arrivé(e)
il était arrivé
elle était arrivée
nous étions arrivé(e)s
vous étiez arrivé(e)(s)
ils étaient arrivés
elles étaient arrivées

PAST CONDITIONAL
conditional of être + past participle

je serais arrivé(e)
tu serais arrivé(e)
il serait arrivé
elle serait arrivée
nous serions arrivé(e)s
vous seriez arrivé(e)(s)
ils seraient arrivés
elles seraient arrivées

PERFECT SUBJUNCTIVE	*PLUPERFECT SUBJUNCTIVE*
present subjunctive of être + past participle	imperfect subjunctive of être + past participle
je sois arrivé(e)	je fusse arrivé(e)
tu sois arrivé(e)	tu fusses arrivé(e)
il soit arrivé	il fût arrivé
elle soit arrivée	elle fût arrivée
nous soyons arrivé(e)s	nous fussions arrivé(e)s
vous soyez arrivé(e)(s)	vous fussiez arrivé(e)(s)
ils soient arrivés	ils fussent arrivés
elles soient arrivées	elles fussent arrivées

4 Avoir or être?

a) *Verbs conjugated with* avoir

The compound tenses of most verbs are formed with avoir:

j'ai marqué un but	elle a dansé toute la nuit
I scored a goal	she danced all night

b) *Verbs conjugated with* être

i) all reflexive verbs (*see* p 116):

je me suis baigné
I had a bath

ii) the following verbs (mainly of motion):

aller	to go
arriver	to arrive
descendre	to go/come down
entrer	to go/come in
monter	to go/come up
mourir	to die
naître	to be born
partir	to leave
passer	to go through, to drop in
rester	to remain
retourner	to return
sortir	to go/come out
tomber	to fall
venir	to come

and most of their compounds:

revenir	to come back
devenir	to become
parvenir	to reach, to manage to
rentrer	to return home
remonter	to go up again
redescendre	to go down again

Note, however, that **prévenir** (to warn) and **subvenir** (to provide for) are conjugated with **avoir**:

je t'avais prévenu!
I did warn you!

elle avait subvenu à toutes les dépenses
she met all the expenses

Note too that **passer** can also be conjugated with **avoir**:

il a passé par Paris
he went via Paris

Some of the verbs listed above can take a direct object. In such cases they are conjugated with **avoir** and will have a different meaning:

descendre	to take/bring down, to go down *(the stairs, a slope)*
monter	to take/bring up, to go up *(the stairs, a slope)*
rentrer	to take/bring/put in
retourner	to turn over
sortir	to take/bring out

les élèves sont sortis à midi
the pupils came out at midday

les élèves ont sorti leurs livres
the pupils took out their books

elle n'est pas encore descendue
she hasn't come down yet

elle a descendu l'escalier
she came down the stairs

elle a descendu un vieux tableau du grenier
she brought an old painting down from the loft

les prisonniers sont montés sur le toit
the prisoners climbed on to the roof

le garçon a monté les bouteilles de vin de la cave
the waiter brought the bottles of wine up from the cellar

nous sommes rentrés tard we got home late	**j'ai rentré la voiture dans le garage** I put the car in the garage
je serais retourné à Paris I would have returned to Paris	**le jardinier a retourné le sol** the gardener turned over the soil
ils sont sortis de la piscine they got out of the swimming pool	**il a sorti les mains de ses poches** he took his hands out of his pockets

 **D REFLEXIVE VERBS**

1 Definition

Reflexive verbs are so called because they 'reflect' the action back onto the subject. Reflexive verbs are always accompanied by a reflexive pronoun, eg in the following sentence:

I look at myself in the mirror

'myself' is the reflexive pronoun.

je lave la voiture I'm washing the car	**je me lave** I'm washing *myself*
j'ai couché le bébé I put the baby to bed	**je me suis couché** I went to bed

2 Reflexive pronouns

They are:

PERSON	SINGULAR	PLURAL
1st	me (m')	nous
	myself	ourselves
2nd	te (t')	vous
	yourself	yourself/selves
3rd	se (s')	se (s')
	himself, herself, itself, oneself	themselves

Note

• M', t' and s' are used instead of me, te and se in front of a vowel or a silent h:

tu t'amuses? – non, je m'ennuie
are you enjoying yourself? – no, I'm bored

il s'habille dans la salle de bain
he gets dressed in the bathroom

• French reflexive pronouns are often not translated in English:

je me demande si ...   **ils se moquent de moi**
I wonder if ...   they're making fun of me

• Plural reflexive pronouns can also be used to express reciprocal actions; in this case they are translated by 'each other' or 'one another':

nous nous détestons   **ils ne se parlent pas**
we hate one another   they're not talking to each other

• Se can mean 'ourselves' or 'each other' when it is used with the pronoun on meaning 'we' (*see* pp 68-9):

on s'est perdu   **on se connaît**
we got lost   we know each other

3 Position of reflexive pronouns

Reflexive pronouns are placed immediately before the verb, except in positive commands, where they follow the verb and are linked to it by a hyphen:

tu te dépêches?	**dépêchons-nous!**
will you hurry up?	let's hurry!
ne t'inquiète pas	**ne vous fiez pas à lui**
don't worry	don't trust him

Note that reflexive pronouns change to emphatic (disjunctive) pronouns in positive commands:

elle doit se reposer	**repose-toi**
she needs to rest	have a rest

4 Conjugation of reflexive verbs

a) *Simple tenses*

These are conjugated in the same way as non-reflexive verbs, except that a reflexive pronoun is used.

b) *Compound tenses*

These are conjugated using the auxiliary être followed by the past participle of the verb.

A full conjugation table is given on **p 183**.

5 Agreement of the past participle

a) In most cases, the reflexive pronoun is a direct object and the past participle of the verb agrees in number and in gender with the reflexive pronoun:

il s'est trompé	**elle s'est endormie**
he made a mistake	she fell asleep
ils se sont excusés	**elles se sont assises**
they apologized	they sat down

b) When the reflexive pronoun is used as an indirect object, the past participle does not change:

nous nous sommes écrit we wrote to each other	**elle se l'est acheté** she bought it for herself
elles se sont parlé they spoke to each other	**les années se sont succédé** one year followed another

When the reflexive verb has a direct object, the reflexive pronoun is the indirect object of the reflexive verb and the past participle does not agree with it:

Caroline s'est tordu la cheville
Caroline sprained her ankle

vous vous êtes lavé les mains, les filles?
did you wash your hands, girls?

elles se sont égratigné les genoux
they scratched their knees

6 Common reflexive verbs

s'en aller (to go away)	**se hâter** (to hurry)
s'amuser (to have fun)	**s'inquiéter** (to worry)
s'appeler (to be called)	**s'installer** (to settle down)
s'approcher (de) (to come near)	**se laver** (to wash)
s'arrêter (to stop)	**se lever** (to get up)
s'asseoir (to sit down)	**se mêler de** (to meddle with)
s'attendre à (to expect)	**se mettre à** (to start)
se baigner (to have a bath)	**se mettre en route** (to set off)
se battre (to fight)	**se moquer de** (to laugh at)
se blesser (to hurt oneself)	**s'occuper de** (to take care of)
se coucher (to go to bed)	**se passer** (to happen)
se débarrasser de (to get rid of)	**se passer de** (to do without)
se demander (to wonder)	**se promener** (to go for a walk)
se dépêcher (to hurry)	**se rappeler** (to remember)

se déshabiller (to undress)	**se raser** (to shave)
se diriger vers (to move towards)	**se renseigner** (to make enquiries)
s'éloigner (de) (to move away (from))	**se ressembler** (to look alike)
s'endormir (to fall asleep)	**se retourner** (to turn round)
s'ennuyer (to be bored)	**se réveiller** (to wake up)
s'étonner (de) (to be surprised (at))	**se sauver** (to run away)
s'excuser (de) (to apologize (for))	**se souvenir (de)** (to remember)
se fâcher (to get angry/fall out)	**se taire** (to be/keep quiet)
s'écrier (to cry out/exclaim)	**se tromper** (to be mistaken)
s'habiller (to get dressed)	**se trouver** (to be (situated))

 E IMPERSONAL VERBS

1 Conjugation

Impersonal verbs are used only in the third person singular and in the infinitive. The subject is always the impersonal pronoun il (= it).

il neige
it's snowing

il y a du brouillard
it's foggy

2 List of impersonal verbs

a) *verbs describing the weather:*

i) faire + adjective:

il fait beau/chaud
it's fine/warm

il fait frais/froid
it's cool/cold

il fera beau demain
it will be a nice day tomorrow

il va faire très froid
it will be very cold

ii) faire + noun:

il fait beau temps
the weather is nice

il fait mauvais temps
the weather is bad

il fait jour
it's daylight

il fait nuit
it's dark

iii) other impersonal verbs and verbs used impersonally to describe the weather:

il gèle	(geler)	it's freezing
il grêle	(grêler)	it's hailing
il neige	(neiger)	it's snowing
il pleut	(pleuvoir)	it's raining
il tonne	(tonner)	there's thunder

Note that some of these verbs may be used personally:

je gèle
I'm freezing

iv) il y a + noun:

il y a des nuages	it's cloudy
il y a du brouillard	it's foggy
il y a du verglas	it's icy

b) être

i) il est + noun:

il est cinq heures	il était une fois un géant
it's five o'clock	once upon a time there was a giant

ii) il est + adjective + de + infinitive:

il est difficile de	it's difficult to
il est facile de	it's easy to
il est nécessaire de	it's necessary to
il est inutile de	it's useless to
il est possible de	it's possible to

il est difficile d'en parler
it's difficult to talk about it

Note that the indirect object pronoun in French corresponds to the English 'for me', 'for him' *etc*:

il m'est difficile d'en parler
it's difficult for me to talk about it

iii) il est + adjective + que:

il est douteux que	it's doubtful that
il est évident que	it's clear that
il est possible que	it's possible that
il est probable que	it's probable that
il est peu probable que	it's unlikely that
il est vrai que	it's true that

Note that que may be followed by the indicative or the subjunctive (*see* p 136):

il est probable qu'il ne viendra pas
he probably won't come

il est peu probable qu'il vienne
it's unlikely that he'll come

c) arriver, se passer *(to happen)*

il est arrivé une chose curieuse
a strange thing happened

que se passe-t-il?
what's happening?

d) exister *(to exist)*, rester *(to remain)*, manquer *(to be missing)*

il existe trois exemplaires de ce livre
there are three copies of this book

il me restait un euro
I had one euro left

il me manque 4 euros
I am 4 euros short

e) paraître, sembler *(to seem)*

il paraîtrait/semblerait qu'il ait changé d'avis
it would appear that he has changed his mind

il paraît qu'il va se marier
it seems he's going to get married

il me semble que le professeur s'est trompé
it seems to me that the teacher has made a mistake

f) *other common impersonal verbs*

i) **s'agir** (to be a matter of) may be followed by a noun, a pronoun or an infinitive:

il s'agit de ton avenir
it's about your future

de quoi s'agit-il?
what's it about?

il s'agit de trouver le coupable
we must find the culprit

ii) **falloir** (to be necessary) may be followed by a noun, an infinitive or the subjunctive:

il faut deux heures pour aller à Paris
it takes two hours to get to Paris

il me faut plus de temps
I need more time

il faut que tu parles à Papa
you have to speak to Dad

il faudra rentrer plus tôt ce soir
we'll have to come home earlier tonight

iii) **suffire** (to be enough) may be followed by a noun, an infinitive or the subjunctive:

il suffit de peu de chose pour être heureux
it doesn't take much to be happy

il suffit de passer le pont
you only have to cross the bridge

il suffira qu'ils te donnent le numéro de téléphone
they will only have to give you the telephone number

iv) **valoir mieux** (to be better) may be followed by an infinitive or the subjunctive:

il vaudrait mieux prendre le car
it would be better to take the coach

il vaut mieux que vous ne sortiez pas seule le soir
you'd better not go out alone at night

TENSES

For the formation of the different tenses, see **pp 98-101** *and* **109-12**.

Note that French has no continuous tenses (as in 'I am eating', 'I was going', 'I will be arriving'). The 'be' and '-ing' parts of English continuous tenses are not translated as separate words. Instead, the equivalent tense is used in French:

je mange	**je mangerai**
I am eating	I will be eating

1 Present

The present is used to describe what someone does/something that happens regularly, or what someone is doing/something that is happening at the time of speaking.

a) *regular actions*

il travaille dans un bureau	**je lis rarement le journal**
he works in an office	I seldom read the paper

b) *continuous actions*

ne le dérangez pas, il travaille
don't disturb him, he's working

je ne peux pas venir, je garde mon petit frère
I can't come, I'm looking after my little brother

Note that the continuous nature of the action can also be expressed by using the phrase **être en train de** (to be in the process of) + infinitive:

je suis en train de cuisiner
I'm (busy) cooking

c) *immediate future*

je pars demain
I'm leaving tomorrow

However, the present cannot be used after quand and other conjunctions of time when the future is implied (*see* pp 125-6):

je le ferai quand j'aurai le temps
I'll do it when I have the time

d) *general truths*

la vie est dure
life is hard

2 Imperfect

The imperfect is a past tense used to express what someone was doing or what someone used to do, or to describe something in the past. The imperfect refers particularly to something that *continued* over a period of time, as opposed to something that happened at a specific point in time.

a) *continuous actions*

the imperfect describes an action that was happening, often when something else took place:

il prenait un bain quand le téléphone a sonné
he was having a bath when the phone rang

excuse-moi, je pensais à autre chose
I'm sorry, I was thinking of something else

Note that the continuous nature of the action can be emphasized by using être en train de + infinitive:

j'étais en train de faire le ménage
I was (busy) doing the housework

b) *regular actions in the past*

je le voyais souvent quand il habitait dans le quartier
I used to see him often when he lived in this area

quand il était plus jeune il voyageait beaucoup
when he was younger he used to travel a lot

c) *description in the past*

il faisait beau ce jour-là	**c'était formidable!**
the weather was good that day	it was great!
elle portait une robe bleue	**elle donnait sur la rue**
she wore a blue dress	it looked onto the street

3 Perfect

The perfect tense is a compound past tense, used to express *single* actions which have been completed. What someone did, has done or has been doing, or something that has happened or has been happening are all expressed using the perfect tense:

je l'ai envoyé lundi	**on est sorti hier soir**
I sent it on Monday	we went out last night
tu t'es bien amusé?	**je ne l'ai pas vu de la journée**
did you have a good time?	I haven't seen him all day
j'ai lu toute la journée	**tu as déjà mangé?**
I've been reading all day	have you eaten?

In English, the simple past ('did', 'went', 'prepared') is used to describe both single and repeated actions in the past. In French, the perfect only describes single actions in the past, while repeated actions are expressed by the imperfect (they are sometimes signposted by 'used to'). Thus 'I went' should be translated 'j'allais' or 'je suis allé' depending on the nature of the action:

après dîner, je suis allé en ville
after dinner I went into town

l'an dernier, j'allais plus souvent au théâtre
last year I went to the theatre more often

4 Past historic

This tense is used in the same way as the perfect tense, to describe a single, completed action in the past (what someone did or something that happened). It is a literary tense, not common in everyday spoken French; it is found mainly as a narrative tense in written form:

> **le piéton ne vit pas arriver la voiture**
> the pedestrian didn't see the car coming

5 Pluperfect

This compound tense is used to express what someone had done/ had been doing or something that had happened or had been happening:

> **il n'avait pas voulu aller avec eux**
> he hadn't wanted to go with them

> **elle était essoufflée parce qu'elle avait couru**
> she was out of breath because she'd been running

However, the pluperfect is not used as in English with depuis (for, since), or with venir de + infinitive (to have just done something). *For details see* pp 127-9:

> **il neigeait depuis une semaine**
> it had been snowing for a week

> **les pompiers venaient d'arriver**
> the firemen had just arrived

6 Future

This tense is used to express what someone will do or will be doing or something that will happen or will be happening:

> **je ferai la vaisselle demain**   **j'arriverai tard**
> I'll do the dishes tomorrow   I'll be arriving late

Note that the future and not the present, as in English, is used in time clauses introduced by quand (when) or other conjunctions of time where the future is implied:

> **il viendra quand il le pourra**
> he'll come when he can

French makes frequent use of aller + infinitive (to be about to do something) to express the immediate future:

je vais vous expliquer ce qui s'est passé
I'll explain (to you) what happened

il va déménager la semaine prochaine
he's moving house next week

7 Future perfect

This compound tense is used to describe what someone will have done or will have been doing in the future or to describe something that will have happened in the future:

j'aurai bientôt fini
I will soon have finished

In particular, it is used instead of the English perfect in time clauses introduced by quand or other conjunctions of time where the future is implied (*see* p 125):

appelle-moi quand tu auras fini
call me when you've finished

on rentrera dès qu'on aura fait les courses
we'll come back as soon as we've done the shopping

8 Past anterior

This tense is used instead of the pluperfect to express an action that preceded another action in the past (ie a past in the past). It is usually introduced by a conjunction of time (translated by 'when', 'as soon as', 'after' *etc*) and the main verb is in the past historic:

il se coucha dès qu'ils furent partis
he went to bed as soon as they'd left

à peine eut-elle raccroché que le téléphone sonna
she'd hardly hung up when the telephone rang

9 Use of tenses with **depuis** (for, since)

a) The present must be used instead of the perfect to describe actions which started in the past and are still continuing:

il habite ici depuis trois ans
he's been living here for three years

elle t'attend depuis ce matin
she's been waiting for you since this morning

Note, however, that the perfect, not the present, is used when the clause is negative or when the action has been completed:

il n'a pas pris de vacances depuis longtemps
he hasn't taken any holidays for a long time

j'ai fini depuis un bon moment
I've been finished for quite a while

> *Note*
>
> • Il y a … que or voilà … que are also used with the present tense to translate 'for':
>
> it's been ringing for ten minutes
> **ça sonne depuis dix minutes**
>
> **il y a dix minutes que ça sonne**
> **voilà dix minutes que ça sonne**
>
> • Depuis que is used when 'since' introduces a clause, ie when there is a verb following depuis:
>
> **elle dort depuis que vous êtes partis**
> she's been sleeping since you left

Note—cont'd

- Do not confuse **depuis** (for, since) and **pendant** (for, during):
  depuis refers to the starting point of an action which is still
  going on and **pendant** refers to the duration of an action which
  is over and is used with the perfect:

  il vit ici depuis deux mois
  he's been living here for two months

  il a vécu ici pendant deux mois
  he lived here for two months

b) The imperfect must be used instead of the pluperfect to describe
   an action which had started in the past and was still going on at
   a given time:

   elle le connaissait depuis son enfance
   she had known him since her childhood

   il attendait depuis trois heures quand on est arrivé
   he had been waiting for three hours when we arrived

   Note, however, that if the sentence is negative or if the action
   has been completed, the pluperfect and not the imperfect is used:

   je n'étais pas allé au théâtre depuis des années
   I hadn't been to the theatre for years

   il était parti depuis peu
   he'd been gone for a short while

Note

- **Il y avait … que** + imperfect is also used to translate 'for':

  she'd been living alone for a long time
  elle habitait seule depuis longtemps
  il y avait longtemps qu'elle habitait seule

Note—cont'd

- **Depuis que** is used when 'since' introduces a clause; if it describes an action which was still going on at the time, it can be followed by the imperfect, otherwise it is followed by the pluperfect:

  il pleuvait depuis que nous étions en vacances
  it had been raining since we had been on holiday

  il pleuvait depuis que nous étions arrivés
  it had been raining since we arrived

- Do not confuse **depuis** and **pendant**: **depuis** refers to the starting point of an action which is still going on and **pendant** refers to the duration of an action which is over; **pendant** is used with the pluperfect:

  j'y travaillais depuis un an
  I had been working there for a year

  j'y avais travaillé pendant un an
  I had worked there for a year

10 Use of tenses with venir de

venir de + infinitive means 'to have just done'.

a) If it describes something that has just happened, it is used in the present instead of the perfect:

   l'avion vient d'arriver   **je viens de te le dire!**
   the plane has just arrived   I've just told you!

b) If it describes something that had just happened, it is used in the imperfect instead of the pluperfect:

   le film venait de commencer   **je venais de rentrer**
   the film had just started   I'd just got home

11 Use of tenses after conjunctions of time

quand	when
tant que	as long as
dès/aussitôt que	as soon as
lorsque	when
pendant que	while

Verbs which follow these conjunctions must be used in the following tenses:

a) *future instead of present:*

je te téléphonerai quand je serai prêt
I'll phone you when I'm ready

elle ira le voir dès qu'elle le pourra
she'll go to see him as soon as she can

b) *future perfect instead of perfect* when the future is implied:

on rentrera dès qu'on aura fini les courses
we'll come back as soon as we've done the shopping

je t'appellerai dès qu'il sera arrivé
I'll call you as soon as he's arrived

c) *conditional present/perfect instead of perfect/pluperfect* in indirect speech:

il a dit qu'il sortirait quand il aurait fini
he said that he would come out when he had finished

For the tenses of the subjunctive and conditional, see pp 130-6 and 138-9.

 G MOODS

1 The subjunctive

In everyday spoken French, the only two subjunctive tenses that are used are the present and the perfect. The imperfect and the pluperfect subjunctive are found mainly in literature or in texts of a formal nature.

The subjunctive is always preceded by the conjunction que and is used in subordinate clauses when the subject of the subordinate clause is different from the subject of the main verb.

Some clauses introduced by que take the indicative. The subjunctive must be used after the following:

a) Verbs of emotion

être content que	to be pleased that
être désolé que	to be sorry that
être étonné que	to be surprised that
être heureux que	to be happy that
être surpris que	to be surprised that
être triste que	to be sad that
avoir peur que ... ne	to be afraid/to fear that
craindre que ... ne	to be afraid/to fear that
regretter que	to be sorry that

ils étaient contents que j'aille les voir
they were pleased (that) I went to visit them

je serais très étonné qu'il mente
I would be very surprised if he was lying

je regrette que tu ne puisses pas y aller
I'm sorry (that) you can't go

Note that ne is used after several verbs in the subjunctive mood but it does not have a negative meaning in itself and is not translated in English:

je crains que l'avion ne soit en retard
I'm afraid (that) the plane will be late

j'ai bien peur qu'il ne soit déjà trop tard
I'm very much afraid (that) it's already too late

pour éviter que la situation ne s'aggrave
to prevent the situation from getting any worse

b) Verbs of wishing and willing:

aimer que	to like
désirer que	to wish (that)
préférer que	to prefer (that)
souhaiter que	to wish (that)
vouloir que	to want

Note that in English, such verbs are often used in the following type of construction: verb of willing + object + infinitive (eg I'd like you to listen); this type of construction is impossible in French, where a subjunctive clause has to be used:

je souhaite que tu réussisses
I hope you will succeed

il aimerait que je lui écrive plus souvent
he'd like me to write to him more often

voulez-vous que je vous y amène en voiture?
would you like me to drive you there?

préférez-vous que je rappelle demain?
would you rather I called back tomorrow?

c) Impersonal constructions (expressing necessity, possibility, doubt, denial, preference):

il faut que	it is necessary (that) *(must)*
il est nécessaire que	it is necessary that *(must)*
il est important que	it is important (that)
il est possible que	it is possible that *(may)*
il se peut que	it is possible that *(may)*
il est impossible que	it is impossible (that) *(can't)*
il est douteux que	it is doubtful whether
il est peu probable que	it is unlikely that
il semble que	it seems (that)
il est préférable que	it is preferable (that)
il vaut mieux que	it is better (that) *(had better)*
c'est dommage que	it is a pity (that)

Note that these expressions may be used in any appropriate tense:

il faut absolument que je le leur dise
I simply must tell them

il était important que tu le saches
it was important that you should know

il se pourrait qu'elle change d'avis
she might change her mind

il est peu probable qu'ils s'y intéressent
they're unlikely to be interested in that

il semble qu'elle ait raison
she appears to be right

il vaudrait mieux que tu ne promettes rien
you'd better not promise anything

c'est dommage que vous vous soyez manqués
it's a pity you missed each other

d) Some verbs and impersonal constructions expressing doubt or uncertainty (mainly used negatively or interrogatively):

douter que	to doubt (that)
(ne pas) croire que	(not) to believe (that)
(ne pas) penser que	(not) to think (that)
(ne pas) être sûr que	(not) to be sure that
il n'est pas certain que	it isn't certain that
il n'est pas évident que	it isn't obvious that
il n'est pas sûr que	it isn't certain that
il n'est pas vrai que	it isn't true that

je doute fort qu'il veuille t'aider
I very much doubt whether he'll want to help you

croyez-vous qu'il y ait des places libres?
do you think there are any seats available?

on n'était pas sûr que ce soit le bon endroit
we weren't sure that it was the right place

il n'était pas certain qu'elle puisse gagner
it wasn't certain whether she could win

e) **attendre que** (to wait until someone does something or something happens, to wait for someone to do something or for something to happen):

attendons qu'il revienne
let's wait until he comes back

f) Some subordinating conjunctions:

bien que	although
quoique	although
sans que	without
pour que	so that
afin que	so that
à condition que	provided that
pourvu que	provided that
jusqu'à ce que	until
en attendant que	until
avant que ... (ne)	before
à moins que ... (ne)	unless
de peur que ... ne	for fear that
de crainte que ... ne	for fear that
de sorte que	so that
de façon que	so that
de manière que	so that

Note that when ne is shown in brackets, it may follow the conjunction, although it is seldom used in spoken French; it does not have a negative meaning, and is not translated in English.

il est allé travailler bien qu'il soit malade
he went to work although he was ill

elle est entrée sans que je la voie
she came in without me seeing her

voilà de l'argent pour que tu puisses aller au cinéma
here's some money so that you can go to the cinema

d'accord, pourvu que tu me promettes de ne pas le répéter
all right, as long as you promise not to tell anyone

tu l'as revu avant qu'il (ne) parte?
did you see him again before he left?

je le ferai demain, à moins que ce (ne) soit urgent
I'll do it tomorrow, unless it's urgent

elle n'a pas fait de bruit de peur qu'il ne se réveille
she didn't make any noise in case he woke

parle moins fort de sorte qu'elle ne nous entende pas
talk more quietly so that she doesn't hear us

Note that when de façon/manière que (so that) expresses a result, as opposed to a purpose, the indicative is used instead of the subjunctive:

il a fait du bruit de sorte qu'elle l'a entendu
he made some noise, and as a result she heard him

g) A superlative or adjectives like premier (first), dernier (last), seul (only) followed by qui or que:

c'était le coureur le plus rapide que j'aie jamais vu
he was the fastest runner I ever saw

Note, however, that the indicative is used with a statement of fact rather than the expression of an opinion:

c'est lui qui me l'a dit
it was he who told me

h) Negative and indefinite pronouns (eg rien, personne, quelqu'un) followed by qui or que:

je ne connais personne qui fasse aussi bien les crêpes
I don't know anyone who can make such good crêpes

il n'y a aucune chance qu'il réussisse
he hasn't got a chance of succeeding

ils cherchent quelqu'un qui puisse garder le bébé
they're looking for someone who can look after the baby

Note, however, that the subjunctive is not used if the verbs in both clauses have the same subject. The infinitive will be used in the subordinate clause instead, sometimes introduced by a preposition (à or de) (*see* pp 142–8).

a) de + infinitive replaces the subjunctive after:

i) verbs of emotion:

j'ai été étonné d'apprendre la nouvelle
I was surprised to hear the news

il regrette de ne pas être arrivé plus tôt
he's sorry he didn't arrive earlier

tu as peur de ne pas avoir assez d'argent?
are you worried you won't have enough money?

ii) attendre (to wait) and douter (to doubt):

j'attendrai d'avoir bu mon café
I'll wait until I've drunk my coffee

iii) most impersonal constructions:

il serait préférable de les en informer tout de suite
it would be better to let them know immediately

il est indispensable de parler une langue étrangère
it's essential to be able to speak a foreign language

iv) most conjunctions:

il est resté dans la voiture afin de ne pas se mouiller
he stayed in the car so as not to get wet

j'ai lu avant de m'endormir
I read before falling asleep

tu peux sortir à condition de rentrer avant minuit
you can go out, as long as you're back before midnight

b) à + infinitive replaces the subjunctive after:

i) de façon/manière

mets la liste sur la table de manière à ne pas l'oublier
put the list on the table so that you won't forget it

ii) premier, seul, dernier

il a été le seul à s'excuser
he was the only one who apologized

c) The infinitive without any linking preposition replaces the subjunctive after:

i) verbs of wishing and willing:

je voudrais sortir avec toi
I'd like to go out with you

ii) il faut, il vaut mieux:

il vous faudra prendre des chèques de voyage
you'll have to take some traveller's cheques

il lui a fallu recommencer à zéro
he had to start all over again

il vaudrait mieux lui apporter des fleurs que des bonbons
it would be better to take her flowers than sweets

Note that il faut + infinitive is used to state a generality. If one particular person *etc* is the subject of the action, an indirect object is used:

il faut réserver à l'avance
you have to book in advance

il lui faut se dépêcher
he has to hurry

iii) verbs of thinking:

je ne crois pas le connaître
I don't think I know him

tu penses être chez toi à cinq heures?
do you think you'll be home at five?

iv) pour and sans:

le car est reparti sans nous attendre
the coach left without waiting for us

j'économise pour pouvoir acheter une moto
I'm saving up to buy a motorbike

2 The conditional

a) The conditional present

   i) The conditional present is used to describe what someone
      would do or would be doing, or what would happen (if
      something else were to happen):

      si j'avais de l'argent, je ferais le tour du monde
      if I had money, I would travel around the world

      Note that when the main verb is in the conditional present, the
      verb after si is in the imperfect.

   ii) It is also used in indirect questions or reported speech instead
      of the future:

      il ne m'a pas dit s'il viendrait
      he didn't tell me whether he *would come*

b) The conditional perfect (or past conditional)
   The conditional perfect or past conditional is used to express
   what someone would have done or would have been doing or
   what would have happened:

   si j'avais su, je n'aurais rien dit
   if I had known, I wouldn't have said anything

   qu'aurais-je fait sans toi?
   what would I have done without you?

   Note that if the main verb is in the conditional perfect, the verb
   introduced by si is in the pluperfect.

c) Tenses after si:
   The tense of the verb introduced by si is determined by the tense
   of the verb in the main clause:

MAIN VERB	VERB FOLLOWING SI
conditional present	imperfect
conditional perfect	pluperfect

je te le dirais si je le savais
I would tell you if I knew

je te l'aurais dit si je l'avais su
I would have told you if I had known

The conditional and the future should never be used with si unless si means 'whether' (ie when it introduces an indirect question):

je me demande si j'y serais arrivé sans toi
I wonder if I would have managed without you

3 The imperative

a) *Definition*

The imperative is used to give commands or polite instructions, or to make requests or suggestions; these can be positive ('do!') or negative ('don't!'):

mange ta soupe!	**n'aie pas peur!**
eat your soup!	don't be afraid!
partons!	**entrez!**
let's go!	come in!
faites attention!	**n'hésitez pas!**
be careful!	don't hesitate!
tournez à droite à la poste	
turn right at the post office	

b) *Forms*

The imperative has only three forms, which are the same as the tu, nous and vous forms of the present tense, but without the subject pronoun:

	-ER verbs	-IR verbs	-RE verbs
'tu' form:	regarde	choisis	attends
	watch	choose	wait
'nous' form:	regardons	choisissons	attendons
	let's watch	let's choose	let's wait
'vous' form:	regardez	choisissez	attendez
	watch	choose	wait

> *Note*
>
> - The -s of the tu form of -er verbs is dropped, except when y or en follow the verb:
>
>   **parle-lui!**
>   speak to him!
>
>   **parles-en avec lui**
>   speak to him about it
>
>   **achète du sucre!**
>   buy some sugar!
>
>   **achètes-en un kilo**
>   buy a kilo (of it)
>
> - The distinction between the subject pronouns tu and vous (*see* p 75) applies to the tu and vous forms of the imperative:
>
>   **prends ta sœur avec toi**
>   take your sister with you
>
>   **prenez le plat du jour, Monsieur; c'est du poulet rôti**
>   have today's special, sir; it's roast chicken
>
>   **ouvrez vos livres à la page 24**
>   open your books at page 24

c) *Negative commands*

In negative commands, the verb is placed between ne and pas (or the second part of other negative expressions):

ne fais pas ça!
don't do that!

ne dites rien!
don't say anything!

d) *Imperative with object pronouns*

In positive commands, object pronouns come after the verb and are attached to it by a hyphen. In negative commands, they come before the verb (*see* pp 77-83):

dites-moi ce qui s'est passé
tell me what happened

ne le leur dis pas!
don't tell them (that)!

attendons-les!
let's wait for them

ne les écoutez pas
don't listen to them

prends-en bien soin, ne l'abîme pas!
take good care of it, don't damage it!

e) *Imperative of reflexive verbs*

The position of the reflexive pronoun of reflexive verbs is the same as that of object pronouns:

tais-toi!
be quiet!

levez-vous!
get up!

méfiez-vous de lui
don't trust him

arrêtons-nous ici
let's stop here

ne nous plaignons pas
let's not complain

ne t'approche pas plus!
don't come any closer!

f) *Alternatives to the imperative*

i) infinitive

the infinitive is often used instead of the imperative in written instructions and in recipes:

s'adresser au concierge
see the caretaker

ne pas fumer
no smoking

verser le lait et bien mélanger
pour in the milk and mix well

ii) subjunctive

as the imperative has no third person (singular or plural), que + subjunctive is used for giving orders in the third person:

qu'il entre!
let him (come) in!

qu'elle parte, je m'en fiche!
I don't care if she goes!

que personne ne me dérange!
don't let anyone disturb me!

g) *Idiomatic usage*

The imperative is used in spoken French in many set phrases. Here are some of the most common ones:

allons donc!
you don't say! hey! *(protest)*

dis/dites donc!
by the way!

tiens/tenez!
here you are!

tiens! voilà le facteur
ah! here comes the postman

tiens (donc)!
(oh) really?

tiens! tiens!
well, well!

voyons!
come (on) now!

voyons donc!
let's see now

 **THE INFINITIVE**

1 The infinitive is the basic form of the verb. It is recognizable by its ending, which is found in three forms corresponding to the three conjugations: -er, -ir, -re.

These endings give the verb the meaning 'to ...':

acheter	**choisir**	**vendre**
to buy	to choose	to sell

Note that although this applies as a general rule, the French infinitive will often be translated by a verbal construction ending in -ing (*see* pp 249-51).

2 Uses of the infinitive

The infinitive can follow a preposition, a verb, a noun, a pronoun, an adverb or an adjective.

a) *After a preposition*

The infinitive can be used after some prepositions (pour, avant de, sans, au lieu de, afin de *etc*):

sans attendre
without waiting

avant de partir
before leaving

b) *After a verb*

There are three main constructions when a verb is followed by an infinitive:

   i) Verbs followed by the infinitive with no linking preposition:
      ❏ verbs of wishing and willing, eg:

vouloir	to want
souhaiter	to wish
désirer	to wish, to want
espérer	to hope

voulez-vous manger maintenant ou plus tard?
do you want to eat now or later?

je souhaite parler au directeur
I wish to speak to the manager

      ❏ verbs of seeing, hearing and feeling, eg:

voir	to see
écouter	to listen to
regarder	to watch
sentir	to feel, to smell
entendre	to hear

je l'ai vu jouer
I've seen him play

tu m'as regardé danser?
did you watch me dance?

j'ai entendu quelqu'un crier
I heard someone shout

❏ verbs of motion, eg:

aller	to go
monter	to go/come up
venir	to come
entrer	to go/come in
rentrer	to go/come home
sortir	to go/come out
descendre	to go/come down

je viendrai te voir demain
I'll come and see you tomorrow

il est descendu laver la voiture
he went down to wash the car

va acheter le journal
go and buy the paper

Note that in English, 'to come' and 'to go' may be linked to the verb that follows by 'and'; 'and' is not translated in French.

❏ aller + infinitive can be used to express a future action:

qu'est-ce que tu vas faire demain?
what are you going to do tomorrow?

❏ modal auxiliary verbs (*see* **pp 158–62**)

❏ verbs of liking and disliking, eg:

aimer	to like
adorer	to love
aimer mieux	to prefer
détester	to hate
préférer	to prefer

tu aimes voyager?
do you like travelling?

j'adore faire la grasse matinée
I love having a lie-in

je déteste aller à la campagne
I hate going to the country

j'aime mieux attendre
I'd rather wait

❏ some impersonal verbs (*see* pp 118-21)

❏ a few other verbs, eg:

compter	to intend to
sembler	to seem
laisser	to let, to allow
faillir	'to nearly' (do)
oser	to dare

ils l'ont laissé partir
they let him go

je n'ose pas le leur demander
I daren't ask them

tu sembles être malade
you seem to be ill

je compte partir demain
I intend to leave tomorrow

j'ai failli manquer l'avion
I nearly missed the plane

❏ in the following set expressions:

aller chercher	to go and get, to fetch
envoyer chercher	to send for
entendre dire (que)	to hear (that)
entendre parler de	to hear about
laisser tomber	to drop
venir chercher	to come and get
vouloir dire	to mean

va chercher ton argent
go and get your money

ne le laisse pas tomber!
don't drop it!

tu as entendu parler de ce film?
have you heard about this film?

ça veut dire 'demain'
it means 'tomorrow'

j'ai entendu dire qu'il était journaliste
I've heard that he's a journalist

ii) Verbs followed by à + infinitive

A list of these is given on pp 197-8:

je dois aider ma mère à préparer le déjeuner
I must help my mother prepare lunch

il commence à faire nuit
it's beginning to get dark

alors, tu t'es décidé à y aller?
so you've made up your mind to go?

je t'invite à venir chez moi pour les vacances de Noël
you are welcome to come to my house for the Christmas holidays

je passe mon temps à lire et à regarder la télé
I spend my time reading and watching TV

cela sert à ouvrir les bouteilles
this is used for opening bottles

iii) Verbs followed by **de** + infinitive

A list of these is given on **pp 198–200**:

je crois qu'il s'est arrêté de pleuvoir
I think it's stopped raining

le médecin a conseillé à Serge de rester au lit
the doctor advised Serge to stay in bed

tu as envie de sortir?
do you feel like going out?

j'ai décidé de rester chez moi
I decided to stay at home

demande à Papa de t'aider
ask Dad to help you

essayons de faire du stop
let's try and hitch-hike

n'oublie pas d'en acheter!
don't forget to buy some!

il vient de téléphoner
he's just phoned

je vous prie de m'excuser
please forgive me

tu as fini de m'ennuyer?
will you stop annoying me?

je t'interdis d'y aller
I forbid you to go

j'ai refusé de le faire
I refused to do it

c) *After a noun, a pronoun, an adverb or an adjective*
There are two possible constructions:

i) with the linking preposition à:

il avait plusieurs clients à voir
he had several customers to see

c'est difficile à dire
it's difficult to say

une maison à vendre
a house for sale

j'ai des examens à préparer
I've got exams to prepare

il nous a indiqué la route à suivre
he showed us the road to follow

il n'y a pas de temps à perdre
there's no time to lose

c'était une occasion à ne pas manquer
it was an opportunity not to be missed

❏ à conveys the idea of something to do or to be done after
the following:

beaucoup	a lot
plus	more
tant	so much
trop	too much
assez	enough
moins	less
rien	nothing
tout	everything
quelque chose	something

il y a trop de livres à lire
there are too many books to read

il n'y a rien à ajouter
there's nothing further to add

elle a quelque chose à nous annoncer
she has something to tell us

❏ à is used in a passive sense (when something is being done)
and after **c'est**:

un livre agréable à lire
a pleasant book to read

il est facile à satisfaire
he is easily satisfied

c'est intéressant à savoir
that's interesting to know

c'était impossible à faire
it was impossible to do

ii) with the linking preposition **de**:

je suis content de te voir
I am pleased to see you

❏ **de** is used after nouns of an abstract nature, usually with the definite article, eg:

l'habitude de	the habit of
l'occasion de	the opportunity to
le temps de	the time to
le courage de	the courage to
l'envie de	the desire to
le besoin de	the need to
le plaisir de	the pleasure of
le moment de	the time to

il n'avait pas l'habitude d'être seul
he wasn't used to being alone

je n'ai pas le temps de leur expliquer
I don't have time to explain it to them

avez-vous eu l'occasion de la rencontrer?
did you have the opportunity to meet her?

ce n'est pas le moment de le déranger
now is not the time to disturb him

je n'ai pas eu le courage de te le dire
I didn't have the courage to tell you

❏ **de** is used after **il est** in an impersonal sense (*see* pp 119-20):

il est intéressant de savoir que ...
it is interesting to know that ...

For information on the use of c'est *and* il est, *see* pp 252-3.

❏ **de** is used after many adjectives, and is frequently used to translate 'of' in English, eg:

certain/sûr de	certain of/to
capable de	capable of
incapable de	incapable of
coupable de	guilty of

j'étais sûr de réussir
I was sure of succeeding

il est incapable d'y arriver seul
he is incapable of managing on his own

❏ **de** is also used with adjectives relating to emotions and states of mind, eg:

content de	pleased/happy to
surpris/étonné de	surprised to
fier de	proud to
heureux de	happy to
fâché de	annoyed to/at
triste de	sad to
gêné de	embarrassed to
désolé de	sorry for/to

j'ai été très content de recevoir ta lettre
I was very pleased to get your letter

elle sera surprise de vous voir
she will be surprised to see you

nous avons été très tristes d'apprendre la nouvelle
we were very sad to hear the news

Note, however, that **à** is used with **prêt à** (ready to) and **disposé à** (willing to):

es-tu prêt à partir?
are you ready to go?

je suis tout disposé à vous aider
I'm very willing to help you

d) faire + infinitive

faire is followed by an infinitive without any linking preposition to express the sense of 'having someone do something' or 'having something done'; two constructions are possible, depending on whether there are one or two objects:

i) when only one object is used, it is a direct object:

je dois le faire réparer
I must have it fixed

il veut faire repeindre sa voiture
he wants to have his car resprayed

cette veste est sale, il faut la faire nettoyer
this jacket's dirty, I'll have to have it cleaned

tu m'as fait attendre!	**je le ferai parler**
you kept me waiting!	I'll make him talk

Note the following set expressions:

faire entrer	**faire venir**
to show in	to send for
faites entrer ce monsieur	**je vais faire venir le docteur**
show this gentleman in	I'll send for the doctor

ii) when both faire and the following infinitive have an object, the object of faire is indirect:

elle m'a fait prendre une douche
she made me take a shower

je leur ai fait ranger leur chambre
I made them tidy their room

e) *Infinitive used as subject of another verb:*

trouver un emploi n'est pas facile
finding a job isn't easy

devenir pilote était mon rêve
my dream was to become a pilot

3 The perfect infinitive

a) *Form*

The perfect or past infinitive is formed with the infinitive of the auxiliary avoir or être as appropriate (*see* pp **109-14**), followed by the past participle of the verb, eg:

avoir mangé	**être allé**	**s'être levé**
to have eaten	to have gone	to have got up

b) *Use*

   i) after the preposition après (after):

   après avoir attendu une heure, il est rentré chez lui
   after waiting for an hour, he went back home

   j'ai compris la remarque après avoir relu le livre
   I understood the remark after reading the book again

   ii) after certain verbs:

se souvenir de	to remember
remercier de	to thank for
regretter de	to regret, to be sorry for
être désolé de	to be sorry for

   je vous remercie de m'avoir invité
   thank you for inviting me

   il regrettait de leur avoir menti
   he was sorry he had lied to them

   tu te souviens d'avoir fait cela?
   do you remember doing this?

 PARTICIPLES

1 The present participle

a) *Formation*

Like the imperfect, the present participle is formed by using the stem of the first person plural of the present tense (the nous

form without the -ons ending) to which -ant (like English -ing)
is added. The following three verbs, however, have irregular
present participles:

INFINITIVE	PRESENT PARTICIPLE
avoir (to have)	ayant (having)
être (to be)	étant (being)
savoir (to know)	sachant (knowing)

b) *Use as an adjective*

Used as an adjective, the present participle agrees in number
and in gender with its noun or pronoun:

un travail fatigant
tiring work

la semaine suivante
the following week

ils sont très exigeants
they're very demanding

des nouvelles surprenantes
surprising news

c) *Use as a verb*

The present participle is used far less frequently in French than
in English, and English present participles in -ing are often not
translated by a participle in French (*see* pp 249-51).

i) Used on its own, the present participle corresponds to the
English present participle:

ne voulant plus attendre, ils sont partis sans moi
not wanting to wait any longer, they left without me

pensant bien faire, j'ai insisté
thinking I was doing the right thing, I insisted

ii) en + present participle

When the subject of the present participle is the same as
that of the main verb, this structure is often used to express
simultaneous actions (ie 'while doing something'), manner

(ie 'by doing something') and to translate English phrasal verbs expressing motion.

❑ simultaneous actions

In English this structure is translated by:

while/when/on + present participle (eg 'on arriving')
while/when/as + subject + verb (eg 'as he arrived')

il est tombé en descendant l'escalier
he fell as he was going down the stairs

en le voyant, j'ai éclaté de rire
when I saw him, I burst out laughing

elle lisait le journal en attendant l'autobus
she was reading the paper while waiting for the bus

Note that the adverb tout is often used before en to emphasize the fact that the actions are simultaneous, especially when there is an element of contradiction:

elle écoutait la radio tout en faisant ses devoirs
she was listening to the radio while doing her homework

tout en protestant, je les ai suivis
under protest, I followed them

❑ manner

When expressing how an action is done, en + participle is translated by 'by' + participle, eg:

il gagne sa vie en vendant des voitures d'occasion
he earns his living (by) selling second-hand cars

j'ai trouvé du travail en lisant les petites annonces
I found a job by reading the classified ads

❑ phrasal verbs of motion

en + present participle is often used to translate English phrasal verbs expressing motion, where the verb expresses the means of motion and a preposition expresses the direction of movement (eg 'to run out', 'to swim across').

In French, the English preposition is translated by a verb, while the English verb is translated by **en** + present participle.

il est sorti du magasin en courant
he *ran* out of the shop

elle a traversé la route en titubant
she *staggered* across the road

2 The past participle

a) *Forms*

For the formation of the past participle see p 109.

b) *Use*

The past participle is mostly used as a verb in compound tenses or in the passive, but it can also be used as an adjective. In either case, there are strict rules of agreement to be followed.

   i) When it is used as an adjective, the past participle always agrees with the noun or pronoun to which it refers:

un pneu crevé	**une pomme pourrie**
a burst tyre	a rotten apple
ils étaient épuisés	**des photos prises à la nuit tombée**
they were exhausted	photos taken at nightfall

Note that in French, the past participle is used as an adjective to describe postures or attitudes of the body, where English uses the present participle. The most common of these are:

accoudé	leaning on one's elbows
accroupi	squatting
agenouillé	kneeling
allongé	lying (down)
appuyé (contre)	leaning (against)
couché	lying (down)
étendu	lying (down)
penché	leaning (over)
(sus)pendu	hanging

il est allongé sur le lit
he's lying on the bed

une femme assise devant moi
a woman sitting in front of me

ii) In compound tenses:

❏ With the auxiliary avoir the past participle agrees in number
and gender with the direct object only when the direct object
comes before the participle, ie in the following cases:

in a clause introduced by the relative pronoun que:

le jeu vidéo que j'ai acheté
the video game I bought

la valise qu'il a perdue
the suitcase he lost

with a direct object pronoun:

je ne trouve pas la disquette; où l'as-tu mise?
I can't find the disk; where did you put it?

merci pour tes suggestions, je les ai trouvées très utiles
thank you for your suggestions; I found them very useful

in a clause introduced by combien de, quel or lequel:

combien de pays as-tu visités?
how many countries have you visited?

laquelle avez-vous choisie?
which one did you choose?

Note that if the direct object comes after the past participle,
the participle remains in the masculine singular form:

on a rencontré des gens très sympathiques
we met some very nice people

❏ With the auxiliary être the past participle agrees with the
subject of the verb:

quand est-elle revenue?
when did she come back?

elle était déjà partie
she'd already left

ils sont passés te voir?
did they come to see you?

elles sont restées là
they stayed here

Note that this rule also applies when the verb is in the passive:

elle a été arrêtée
she's been arrested

❏ With reflexive verbs the past participle normally agrees with the reflexive pronoun if the pronoun is a direct object; since the reflexive pronoun refers to the subject, the number and gender of the past participle are determined by the subject:

Jacques s'est trompé	**Marie s'était levée tard**
Jacques made a mistake	Marie had got up late
ils se sont disputés?	**elles se sont vues**
did they have an argument?	they saw each other

Michèle et Marie, vous vous êtes habillées?
Michèle and Marie, have you got dressed yet?

Note, however, that the past participle does not agree when the reflexive pronoun is an indirect object:

elles se sont écrit	**elle s'est lavé les cheveux**
they wrote *to* each other	she washed her hair
ils se sont serré la main	
they shook hands	

 THE PASSIVE

1 Formation

The passive is used when the subject does not perform the action, but is subjected to it, eg:

the house has been sold

he was made redundant

Passive tenses are formed with the corresponding tense of the verb 'être' ('to be', as in English), followed by the past participle of the verb, eg:

j'ai été invité
I was invited

The past participle must agree with its subject, eg:

il sera puni
he will be punished

ils seront déçus
they will be disappointed

elle a été renvoyée
she has been dismissed

elles ont été vues
they were seen

2 Avoidance of the passive

The passive is far less common in French than in English. In particular, an indirect object cannot become the subject of a sentence in French; the following sentence, where 'he' is an indirect object, has no equivalent in French:

he was given a book *(ie a book was given to him)*

In general, French tries to avoid the passive wherever possible. This can be done in several ways.

a) *By using the pronoun* on:

on m'a volé mon portefeuille
my wallet has been stolen

on construit une nouvelle piscine
a new swimming pool is being built

en France, on boit beaucoup de vin
a lot of wine is drunk in France

b) *By making the agent the subject of the verb*

If the agent, that is the real subject, is mentioned in English, it can become the subject of the French verb:

la nouvelle va les surprendre   **mon correspondant m'a invité**
they will be surprised by *the news*   I've been invited by *my penfriend*

mon cadeau te plaît?
are you pleased with *my present*?

c) *By using a reflexive verb*

Reflexive forms can be created for a large number of verbs, particularly in the third person:

elle s'appelle Anne   **ton absence va se remarquer**
she is called Anne   your absence will be noticed

ce plat se mange froid   **cela ne se fait pas ici**
this dish is eaten cold   that isn't done here

d) *By using* **se faire** + *infinitive (when the subject is a person)*

il s'est fait renverser par une voiture
he was run over by a car

je me suis fait couper les cheveux
I've had my hair cut

3 Conjugation

For the complete conjugation of a verb in the passive, see **être aimé** (to be loved), p 166.

 ## K MODAL AUXILIARY VERBS

The modal auxiliary verbs are always followed by the infinitive. They express an obligation, a probability, an intention, a possibility or a wish rather than a fact.

The five modal auxiliary verbs are: **devoir, pouvoir, savoir, vouloir** and **falloir**.

1 Devoir (*for conjugation see* p 174) is used to express the following:

a) *Obligation*

nous devons arriver à temps
we must arrive in time

nous avions dû partir
we had (had) to go

demain tu devras prendre le bus
tomorrow you'll have to take the bus

j'ai dû avouer que j'avais tort
I had to admit that I was wrong

In the conditional, devoir may be used for advice, ie to express what should be done (conditional present) or should have been done (conditional past):

vous devriez travailler davantage
you ought to/should work harder

tu ne devrais pas marcher sur l'herbe
you shouldn't walk on the grass

tu aurais dû tout avouer
you should have admitted everything

tu n'aurais pas dû manger ces champignons
you shouldn't have eaten those mushrooms

Note that the French infinitive is translated by a past participle in English: man**ger** = eat**en**.

b) *Probability*

il doit être en train de dormir
he must be sleeping (he's probably sleeping)

j'ai dû me tromper de chemin
I must have taken the wrong road

Note that in a past narrative sequence in the distant past, 'must have' is translated by a pluperfect in French:

il dit qu'il avait dû se tromper de chemin
he said he must have taken the wrong road

c) *Intention, expectation*

je dois aller chez le dentiste
I am supposed to go to the dentist

le train doit arriver à 19h30
the train is due to arrive at 7.30p.m.

2 Pouvoir (*for conjugation see* p 186) is used to express the following:

a) *Capacity/ability*

il peut rester plusieurs jours sans dormir
he can go without sleep for several days

cette voiture peut faire du 150
this car can go up to 93 mph

il était si faible qu'il ne pouvait pas sortir de son lit
he was so weak that he couldn't get out of bed

b) *Permission*

puis-je entrer?
may I come in?

puis-je vous offrir du thé?
may I offer you some tea?

c) *Possibility*

cela peut arriver
it can happen

ça peut n'avoir aucune importance
it might not be at all important

Note that pouvoir + the infinitive is usually replaced by peut-être + the finite tense, eg il s'est peut-être trompé de livres (he may have taken the wrong books).

In the conditional, pouvoir is used to express something that could or might be (conditional present) or that could or might have been (conditional past):

tu pourrais t'excuser
you might apologize

j'aurais pu vous prêter mon téléphone portable
I could have lent you my mobile phone

Note that with verbs of perception, eg **entendre** (to hear), **sentir** (to feel, to smell), **voir** (to see), **pouvoir** is often omitted.

j'entendais le bruit des vagues
I could hear the sound of the waves

3 Savoir (*for conjugation see* p 189) is used to express 'to know how to':

je sais/savais conduire une moto
I can/used to be able to ride a motorbike

elle sait parler plusieurs langues
she can speak several languages

4 Vouloir (*for conjugation see* p 195) is used to express the following:

a) *Desire*

je veux partir   **voulez-vous danser avec moi?**
I want to go   will you dance with me?

b) *Wish*

je voudrais être riche
I wish I were rich

je voudrais trouver un travail intéressant
I'd like to find an interesting job

j'aurais voulu te donner un coup de poing
I would have liked to punch you

c) *Intention*

il a voulu sauter par la fenêtre
he tried to jump out of the window

Note that **veuillez**, the imperative of vouloir, is used as a polite form to express a request ('would you please ...'):

veuillez ne pas déranger
please do not disturb

5 Falloir (*for conjugation see* p 181) is used to express necessity:

il faut manger pour vivre	il faudrait y aller tout de suite
you must eat to live	we should go right away

il aurait fallu apporter des sandwichs
we should have brought sandwiches

Note that some of the above verbs can also be used without infinitive constructions in which case they have a different meaning, eg devoir = to owe, savoir = to know.

je te dois 20 euros	elle le sait par cœur
I owe you 20 euros	she knows it by heart

 L CONJUGATION TABLES

The following verbs provide the main patterns of conjugation including the conjugation of the most common irregular verbs. They are arranged in alphabetical order:

-er verb (*see* p 99)	AIMER
-ir verb (*see* p 99)	FINIR
-re verb (*see* p 99)	VENDRE
Reflexive verb (*see* pp 114-8)	SE MÉFIER
Verb with auxiliary être (*see* pp 112-4)	ARRIVER
Verb in the passive (*see* pp 156-8)	ÊTRE AIMÉ
Auxiliaries (*see* pp 109-14)	AVOIR
	ÊTRE
Verb ending in -eler/-eter (*see* pp 103-5)	APPELER
Verb ending in -e + consonant + er (*see* pp 106-7)	ACHETER
Verb ending in é + consonant + er (*see* pp 107-8)	ESPÉRER
Modal auxiliaries (*see* pp 158-62)	DEVOIR
	POUVOIR
	SAVOIR
	VOULOIR
	FALLOIR

Irregular verbs	ALLER	METTRE
	CONDUIRE	OUVRIR
	CONNAÎTRE	PRENDRE
	CROIRE	RECEVOIR
	DIRE	TENIR
	DORMIR	VENIR
	ÉCRIRE	VIVRE
	FAIRE	VOIR

'Chambers French Verbs', a fully comprehensive list of French verbs and their conjugations, is also available in this series.

ACHETER *to buy*

PRESENT	IMPERFECT	FUTURE
j'achète	j'achetais	j'achèterai
tu achètes	tu achetais	tu achèteras
il achète	il achetait	il achètera
nous achetons	nous achetions	nous achèterons
vous achetez	vous achetiez	vous achèterez
ils achètent	ils achetaient	ils achèteront

PAST HISTORIC	PERFECT	PLUPERFECT
j'achetai	j'ai acheté	j'avais acheté
tu achetas	tu as acheté	tu avais acheté
il acheta	il a acheté	il avait acheté
nous achetâmes	nous avons acheté	nous avions acheté
vous achetâtes	vous avez acheté	vous aviez acheté
ils achetèrent	ils ont acheté	ils avaient acheté

CONDITIONAL

	PRESENT	PAST
PAST ANTERIOR	j'achèterais	j'aurais acheté
j'eus acheté *etc*	tu achèterais	tu aurais acheté
	il achèterait	il aurait acheté
	nous achèterions	nous aurions acheté
FUTURE PERFECT	vous achèteriez	vous auriez acheté
j'aurai acheté *etc*	ils achèteraient	ils auraient acheté

SUBJUNCTIVE

PRESENT	IMPERFECT	PERFECT
j'achète	j'achetasse	j'aie acheté
tu achètes	tu achetasses	tu aies acheté
il achète	il achetât	il ait acheté
nous achetions	nous achetassions	nous ayons acheté
vous achetiez	vous achetassiez	vous ayez acheté
ils achètent	ils achetassent	ils aient acheté

IMPERATIVE / INFINITIVE / PARTICIPLE

IMPERATIVE	INFINITIVE	PARTICIPLE
achète	PRESENT	PRESENT
achetons	acheter	achetant
achetez		
	PAST	PAST
	avoir acheté	acheté

AIMER *to like/to love*

PRESENT	IMPERFECT	FUTURE
j'aime	j'aimais	j'aimerai
tu aimes	tu aimais	tu aimeras
il aime	il aimait	il aimera
nous aimons	nous aimions	nous aimerons
vous aimez	vous aimiez	vous aimerez
ils aiment	ils aimaient	ils aimeront

PAST HISTORIC	PERFECT	PLUPERFECT
j'aimai	j'ai aimé	j'avais aimé
tu aimas	tu as aimé	tu avais aimé
il aima	il a aimé	il avait aimé
nous aimâmes	nous avons aimé	nous avions aimé
vous aimâtes	vous avez aimé	vous aviez aimé
ils aimèrent	ils ont aimé	ils avaient aimé

CONDITIONAL

PAST ANTERIOR	PRESENT	PAST
j'eus aimé *etc*	j'aimerais	j'aurais aimé
	tu aimerais	tu aurais aimé
	il aimerait	il aurait aimé
	nous aimerions	nous aurions aimé
FUTURE PERFECT	vous aimeriez	vous auriez aimé
j'aurai aimé *etc*	ils aimeraient	ils auraient aimé

SUBJUNCTIVE

PRESENT	IMPERFECT	PERFECT
j'aime	j'aimasse	j'aie aimé
tu aimes	tu aimasses	tu aies aimé
il aime	il aimât	il ait aimé
nous aimions	nous aimassions	nous ayons aimé
vous aimiez	vous aimassiez	vous ayez aimé
ils aiment	ils aimassent	ils aient aimé

IMPERATIVE

IMPERATIVE	INFINITIVE	PARTICIPLE
aime	PRESENT	PRESENT
aimons	aimer	aimant
aimez		
	PAST	PAST
	avoir aimé	aimé

ÊTRE AIMÉ to be loved

PRESENT	IMPERFECT	FUTURE
je suis aimé(e)	j'étais aimé(e)	je serai aimé(e)
tu es aimé(e)	tu étais aimé(e)	tu seras aimé(e)
il (elle) est aimé(e)	il (elle) était aimé(e)	il (elle) sera aimé(e)
nous sommes aimé(e)s	nous étions aimé(e)s	nous serons aimé(e)s
vous êtes aimé(e)(s)	vous étiez aimé(e)(s)	vous serez aimé(e)(s)
ils (elles) sont aimé(e)s	ils (elles) étaient aimé(e)s	ils seront aimé(e)s

PAST HISTORIC	PERFECT	PLUPERFECT
je fus aimé(e)	j'ai été aimé(e)	j'avais été aimé(e)
tu fus aimé(e)	tu as été aimé(e)	tu avais été aimé(e)
il (elle) fut aimé(e)	il (elle) a été aimé(e)	il (elle) avait été aimé(e)
nous fûmes aimé(e)s	nous avons été aimé(e)s	nous avions été aimé(e)s
vous fûtes aimé(e)(s)	vous avez été aimé(e)(s)	vous aviez été aimé(e)s
ils (elles) furent aimé(e)s	ils (elles) ont été aimé(e)s	ils (elles) avaient été aimé(e)s

CONDITIONAL

	PRESENT	PAST
PAST ANTERIOR	je serais aimé(e)	j'aurais été aimé(e)
j'eus été aimé(e) *etc*	tu serais aimé(e)	tu aurais été aimé(e)
	il (elle) serait aimé(e)	il (elle) aurait été aimé(e)
	nous serions aimé(e)s	nous aurions été aimé(e)s
FUTURE PERFECT	vous seriez aimé(e)(s)	vous auriez été aimé(e)(s)
j'aurai été aimé(e) *etc*	ils (elles) seraient aimé(e)s	ils (elles) auraient été aimé(e)s

SUBJUNCTIVE

PRESENT	IMPERFECT	PERFECT
je sois aimé(e)	je fusse aimé(e)	j'aie été aimé(e)
tu sois aimé(e)	tu fusses aimé(e)	tu aies été aimé(e)
il (elle) soit aimé(e)	il (elle) fût aimé(e)	il (elle) ait été aimé(e)
nous soyons aimé(e)s	nous fussions aimé(e)s	nous ayons été aimé(e)s
vous soyez aimé(e)(s)	vous fussiez aimé(e)(s)	vous ayez été aimé(e)(s)
ils (elles) soient aimé(e)s	ils (elles) fussent aimé(e)s	ils (elles) aient été aimé(e)s

IMPERATIVE / INFINITIVE / PARTICIPLE

IMPERATIVE	INFINITIVE	PARTICIPLE
sois aimé(e)	**PRESENT**	**PRESENT**
soyons aimé(e)s	être aimé(e)(s)	étant aimé(e)(s)
soyez aimé(e)(s)		
	PAST	**PAST**
	avoir été aimé(e)(s)	été aimé(e)(s)

ALLER *to go*

PRESENT	IMPERFECT	FUTURE
je vais	j'allais	j'irai
tu vas	tu allais	tu iras
il va	il allait	il ira
nous allons	nous allions	nous irons
vous allez	vous alliez	vous irez
ils vont	ils allaient	ils iront

PAST HISTORIC	PERFECT	PLUPERFECT
j'allai	je suis allé(e)	j'étais allé(e)
tu allas	tu es allé(e)	tu étais allé(e)
il alla	il (elle) est allé(e)	il (elle) était allé(e)
nous allâmes	nous sommes allé(e)s	nous étions allé(e)s
vous allâtes	vous êtes allé(e)(s)	vous étiez allé(e)(s)
ils allèrent	ils (elles) sont allé(e)s	ils (elles) étaient allé(e)s

CONDITIONAL

PAST ANTERIOR	PRESENT	PAST
je fus allé(e) *etc*	j'irais	je serais allé(e)
	tu irais	tu serais allé(e)
	il irait	il (elle) serait allé(e)
	nous irions	nous serions allé(e)s
FUTURE PERFECT	vous iriez	vous seriez allé(e)(s)
je serai allé(e) *etc*	ils iraient	ils (elles) seraient allé(e)s

SUBJUNCTIVE

PRESENT	IMPERFECT	PERFECT
j'aille	j'allasse	je sois allé(e)
tu ailles	tu allasses	tu sois allé(e)
il aille	il allât	il (elle) soit allé(e)
nous allions	nous allassions	nous soyons allé(e)s
vous alliez	vous allassiez	vous soyez allé(e)(s)
ils aillent	ils allassent	ils (elles) soient allé(e)s

IMPERATIVE	INFINITIVE	PARTICIPLE
va	PRESENT	PRESENT
allons	aller	allant
allez		
	PAST	PAST
	être allé(e)(s)	allé

APPELER *to call*

PRESENT	IMPERFECT	FUTURE
j'appelle	j'appelais	j'appellerai
tu appelles	tu appelais	tu appelleras
il appelle	il appelait	il appellera
nous appelons	nous appelions	nous appellerons
vous appelez	vous appeliez	vous appellerez
ils appellent	ils appelaient	ils appelleront

PAST HISTORIC	PERFECT	PLUPERFECT
j'appelai	j'ai appelé	j'avais appelé
tu appelas	tu as appelé	tu avais appelé
il appela	il a appelé	il avait appelé
nous appelâmes	nous avons appelé	nous avions appelé
vous appelâtes	vous avez appelé	vous aviez appelé
ils appelèrent	ils ont appelé	ils avaient appelé

CONDITIONAL

PAST ANTERIOR	PRESENT	PAST
j'eus appelé *etc*	j'appellerais	j'aurais appelé
	tu appellerais	tu aurais appelé
	il appellerait	il aurait appelé
	nous appellerions	nous aurions appelé
FUTURE PERFECT	vous appelleriez	vous auriez appelé
j'aurai appelé *etc*	ils appelleraient	ils auraient appelé

SUBJUNCTIVE

PRESENT	IMPERFECT	PERFECT
j'appelle	j'appelasse	j'aie appelé
tu appelles	tu appelasses	tu aies appelé
il appelle	il appelât	il ait appelé
nous appelions	nous appelassions	nous ayons appelé
vous appeliez	vous appelassiez	vous ayez appelé
ils appellent	ils appelassent	ils aient appelé

IMPERATIVE / INFINITIVE / PARTICIPLE

IMPERATIVE	INFINITIVE	PARTICIPLE
appelle	PRESENT	PRESENT
appelons	appeler	appelant
appelez		
	PAST	PAST
	avoir appelé	appelé

ARRIVER *to arrive; to happen*

PRESENT	**IMPERFECT**	**FUTURE**
j'arrive	j'arrivais	j'arriverai
tu arrives	tu arrivais	tu arriveras
il arrive	il arrivait	il arrivera
nous arrivons	nous arrivions	nous arriverons
vous arrivez	vous arriviez	vous arriverez
ils arrivent	ils arrivaient	ils arriveront

PAST HISTORIC	**PERFECT**	**PLUPERFECT**
j'arrivai	je suis arrivé(e)	j'étais arrivé(e)
tu arrivas	tu es arrivé(e)	tu étais arrivé(e)
il arriva	il (elle) est arrivé(e)	il (elle) était arrivé(e)
nous arrivâmes	nous sommes arrivé(e)s	nous étions arrivé(e)s
vous arrivâtes	vous êtes arrivé(e)(s)	vous étiez arrivé(e)(s)
ils arrivèrent	ils (elles) sont arrivé(e)s	ils (elles) étaient arrivé(e)s

CONDITIONAL

PAST ANTERIOR	**PRESENT**	**PAST**
je fus arrivé(e) *etc*	j'arriverais	je serais arrivé(e)
	tu arriverais	tu serais arrivé(e)
	il arriverait	il (elle) serait arrivé(e)
	nous arriverions	nous serions arrivé(e)s
FUTURE PERFECT	vous arriveriez	vous seriez arrivé(e)(s)
je serai arrivé(e) *etc*	ils arriveraient	ils (elles) seraient arrivé(e)s

SUBJUNCTIVE

PRESENT	**IMPERFECT**	**PERFECT**
j'arrive	j'arrivasse	je sois arrivé(e)
tu arrives	tu arrivasses	tu sois arrivé(e)
il arrive	il arrivât	il (elle) soit arrivé(e)
nous arrivions	nous arrivassions	nous soyons arrivé(e)s
vous arriviez	vous arrivassiez	vous soyez arrivé(e)(s)
ils arrivent	ils arrivassent	ils (elles) soient arrivé(e)s

IMPERATIVE	*INFINITIVE*	*PARTICIPLE*
arrive	**PRESENT**	**PRESENT**
arrivons	arriver	arrivant
arrivez		
	PAST	**PAST**
	être arrivé(e)(s)	arrivé

AVOIR *to have*

PRESENT	IMPERFECT	FUTURE
j'ai	j'avais	j'aurai
tu as	tu avais	tu auras
il a	il avait	il aura
nous avons	nous avions	nous aurons
vous avez	vous aviez	vous aurez
ils ont	ils avaient	ils auront

PAST HISTORIC	PERFECT	PLUPERFECT
j'eus	j'ai eu	j'avais eu
tu eus	tu as eu	tu avais eu
il eut	il a eu	il avait eu
nous eûmes	nous avons eu	nous avions eu
vous eûtes	vous avez eu	vous aviez eu
ils eurent	ils ont eu	ils avaient eu

CONDITIONAL

PAST ANTERIOR	PRESENT	PAST
j'eus eu *etc*	j'aurais	j'aurais eu
	tu aurais	tu aurais eu
	il aurait	il aurait eu
	nous aurions	nous aurions eu
FUTURE PERFECT	vous auriez	vous auriez eu
j'aurai eu *etc*	ils auraient	ils auraient eu

SUBJUNCTIVE

PRESENT	IMPERFECT	PERFECT
j'aie	j'eusse	j'aie eu
tu aies	tu eusses	tu aies eu
il ait	il eût	il ait eu
nous ayons	nous eussions	nous ayons eu
vous ayez	vous eussiez	vous ayez eu
ils aient	ils eussent	ils aient eu

IMPERATIVE · INFINITIVE · PARTICIPLE

IMPERATIVE	INFINITIVE	PARTICIPLE
aie	**PRESENT**	**PRESENT**
ayons	avoir	ayant
ayez		
	PAST	**PAST**
	avoir eu	eu

CONDUIRE *to lead; to drive*

PRESENT	IMPERFECT	FUTURE
je conduis	je conduisais	je conduirai
tu conduis	tu conduisais	tu conduiras
il conduit	il conduisait	il conduira
nous conduisons	nous conduisions	nous conduirons
vous conduisez	vous conduisiez	vous conduirez
ils conduisent	ils conduisaient	ils conduiront

PAST HISTORIC	PERFECT	PLUPERFECT
je conduisis	j'ai conduit	j'avais conduit
tu conduisis	tu as conduit	tu avais conduit
il conduisit	il a conduit	il avait conduit
nous conduisîmes	nous avons conduit	nous avions conduit
vous conduisîtes	vous avez conduit	vous aviez conduit
ils conduisirent	ils ont conduit	ils avaient conduit

CONDITIONAL

PAST ANTERIOR	PRESENT	PAST
j'eus conduit *etc*	je conduirais	j'aurais conduit
	tu conduirais	tu aurais conduit
	il conduirait	il aurait conduit
	nous conduirions	nous aurions conduit
FUTURE PERFECT	vous conduiriez	vous auriez conduit
j'aurai conduit *etc*	ils conduiraient	ils auraient conduit

SUBJUNCTIVE

PRESENT	IMPERFECT	PERFECT
je conduise	je conduisisse	j'aie conduit
tu conduises	tu conduisisses	tu aies conduit
il conduise	il conduisît	il ait conduit
nous conduisions	nous conduisissions	nous ayons conduit
vous conduisiez	vous conduisissiez	vous ayez conduit
ils conduisent	ils conduisissent	ils aient conduit

IMPERATIVE	INFINITIVE	PARTICIPLE
conduis	PRESENT	PRESENT
conduisons	conduire	conduisant
conduisez		
	PAST	PAST
	avoir conduit	conduit

CONNAÎTRE *to know*

PRESENT
je connais
tu connais
il connaît
nous connaissons
vous connaissez
ils connaissent

IMPERFECT
je connaissais
tu connaissais
il connaissait
nous connaissions
vous connaissiez
ils connaissaient

FUTURE
je connaîtrai
tu connaîtras
il connaîtra
nous connaîtrons
vous connaîtrez
ils connaîtront

PAST HISTORIC
je connus
tu connus
il connut
nous connûmes
vous connûtes
ils connurent

PERFECT
j'ai connu
tu as connu
il a connu
nous avons connu
vous avez connu
ils ont connu

PLUPERFECT
j'avais connu
tu avais connu
il avait connu
nous avions connu
vous aviez connu
ils avaient connu

CONDITIONAL

PAST ANTERIOR
j'eus connu *etc*

FUTURE PERFECT
j'aurai connu *etc*

PRESENT
je connaîtrais
tu connaîtrais
il connaîtrait
nous connaîtrions
vous connaîtriez
ils connaîtraient

PAST
j'aurais connu
tu aurais connu
il aurait connu
nous aurions connu
vous auriez connu
ils auraient connu

SUBJUNCTIVE

PRESENT
je connaisse
tu connaisses
il connaisse
nous connaissions
vous connaissiez
ils connaissent

IMPERFECT
je connusse
tu connusses
il connût
nous connussions
vous connussiez
ils connussent

PERFECT
j'aie connu
tu aies connu
il ait connu
nous ayons connu
vous ayez connu
ils aient connu

IMPERATIVE

connais
connaissons
connaissez

INFINITIVE

PRESENT
connaître

PAST
avoir connu

PARTICIPLE

PRESENT
connaissant

PAST
connu

CROIRE *to believe*

PRESENT	IMPERFECT	FUTURE
je crois	je croyais	je croirai
tu crois	tu croyais	tu croiras
il croit	il croyait	il croira
nous croyons	nous croyions	nous croirons
vous croyez	vous croyiez	vous croirez
ils croient	ils croyaient	ils croiront

PAST HISTORIC	PERFECT	PLUPERFECT
je crus	j'ai cru	j'avais cru
tu crus	tu as cru	tu avais cru
il crut	il a cru	il avait cru
nous crûmes	nous avons cru	nous avions cru
vous crûtes	vous avez cru	vous aviez cru
ils crurent	ils ont cru	ils avaient cru

CONDITIONAL

PAST ANTERIOR	PRESENT	PAST
j'eus cru *etc*	je croirais	j'aurais cru
	tu croirais	tu aurais cru
	il croirait	il aurait cru
	nous croirions	nous aurions cru
FUTURE PERFECT	vous croiriez	vous auriez cru
j'aurai cru *etc*	ils croiraient	ils auraient cru

SUBJUNCTIVE

PRESENT	IMPERFECT	PERFECT
je croie	je crusse	j'aie cru
tu croies	tu crusses	tu aies cru
il croie	il crût	il ait cru
nous croyions	nous crussions	nous ayons cru
vous croyiez	vous crussiez	vous ayez cru
ils croient	ils crussent	ils aient cru

IMPERATIVE	INFINITIVE	PARTICIPLE
crois	PRESENT	PRESENT
croyons	croire	croyant
croyez		
	PAST	PAST
	avoir cru	cru

DEVOIR *to owe; to have to*

PRESENT	IMPERFECT	FUTURE
je dois	je devais	je devrai
tu dois	tu devais	tu devras
il doit	il devait	il devra
nous devons	nous devions	nous devrons
vous devez	vous deviez	vous devrez
ils doivent	ils devaient	ils devront

PAST HISTORIC	PERFECT	PLUPERFECT
je dus	j'ai dû	j'avais dû
tu dus	tu as dû	tu avais dû
il dut	il a dû	il avait dû
nous dûmes	nous avons dû	nous avions dû
vous dûtes	vous avez dû	vous aviez dû
ils durent	ils ont dû	ils avaient dû

CONDITIONAL

PAST ANTERIOR	PRESENT	PAST
j'eus dû *etc*	je devrais	j'aurais dû
	tu devrais	tu aurais dû
	il devrait	il aurait dû
	nous devrions	nous aurions dû
FUTURE PERFECT	vous devriez	vous auriez dû
j'aurai dû	ils devraient	ils auraient dû

SUBJUNCTIVE

PRESENT	IMPERFECT	PERFECT
je doive	je dusse	j'aie dû
tu doives	tu dusses	tu aies dû
il doive	il dût	il ait dû
nous devions	nous dussions	nous ayons dû
vous deviez	vous dussiez	vous ayez dû
ils doivent	ils dussent	ils aient dû

IMPERATIVE | INFINITIVE | PARTICIPLE

IMPERATIVE	INFINITIVE	PARTICIPLE
dois	**PRESENT**	**PRESENT**
devons	devoir	devant
devez		
	PAST	**PAST**
	avoir dû	dû (due, dus)

DIRE *to say*

PRESENT	IMPERFECT	FUTURE
je dis	je disais	je dirai
tu dis	tu disais	tu diras
il dit	il disait	il dira
nous disons	nous disions	nous dirons
vous dites	vous disiez	vous direz
ils disent	ils disaient	ils diront

PAST HISTORIC	PERFECT	PLUPERFECT
je dis	j'ai dit	j'avais dit
tu dis	tu as dit	tu avais dit
il dit	il a dit	il avait dit
nous dîmes	nous avons dit	nous avions dit
vous dîtes	vous avez dit	vous aviez dit
ils dirent	ils ont dit	ils avaient dit

CONDITIONAL

PAST ANTERIOR	PRESENT	PAST
j'eus dit *etc*	je dirais	j'aurais dit
	tu dirais	tu aurais dit
	il dirait	il aurait dit
	nous dirions	nous aurions dit
FUTURE PERFECT	vous diriez	vous auriez dit
j'aurai dit *etc*	ils diraient	ils auraient dit

SUBJUNCTIVE

PRESENT	IMPERFECT	PERFECT
je dise	je disse	j'aie dit
tu dises	tu disses	tu aies dit
il dise	il dît	il ait dit
nous disions	nous dissions	nous ayons dit
vous disiez	vous dissiez	vous ayez dit
ils disent	ils dissent	ils aient dit

IMPERATIVE	INFINITIVE	PARTICIPLE
dis	**PRESENT**	**PRESENT**
disons	dire	disant
dites		
	PAST	**PAST**
	avoir dit	dit

DORMIR *to sleep*

PRESENT	IMPERFECT	FUTURE
je dors	je dormais	je dormirai
tu dors	tu dormais	tu dormiras
il dort	il dormait	il dormira
nous dormons	nous dormions	nous dormirons
vous dormez	vous dormiez	vous dormirez
ils dorment	ils dormaient	ils dormiront

PAST HISTORIC	PERFECT	PLUPERFECT
je dormis	j'ai dormi	j'avais dormi
tu dormis	tu as dormi	tu avais dormi
il dormit	il a dormi	il avait dormi
nous dormîmes	nous avons dormi	nous avions dormi
vous dormîtes	vous avez dormi	vous aviez dormi
ils dormirent	ils ont dormi	ils avaient dormi

CONDITIONAL

PAST ANTERIOR	PRESENT	PAST
j'eus dormi *etc*	je dormirais	j'aurais dormi
	tu dormirais	tu aurais dormi
	il dormirait	il aurait dormi
	nous dormirions	nous aurions dormi
FUTURE PERFECT	vous dormiriez	vous auriez dormi
j'aurai dormi *etc*	ils dormiraient	ils auraient dormi

SUBJUNCTIVE

PRESENT	IMPERFECT	PERFECT
je dorme	je dormisse	j'aie dormi
tu dormes	tu dormisses	tu aies dormi
il dorme	il dormît	il ait dormi
nous dormions	nous dormissions	nous ayons dormi
vous dormiez	vous dormissiez	vous ayez dormi
ils dorment	ils dormissent	ils aient dormi

IMPERATIVE / INFINITIVE / PARTICIPLE

IMPERATIVE	INFINITIVE	PARTICIPLE
dors	PRESENT	PRESENT
dormons	dormir	dormant
dormez		
	PAST	PAST
	avoir dormi	dormi

ÉCRIRE *to write*

PRESENT	IMPERFECT	FUTURE
j'écris	j'écrivais	j'écrirai
tu écris	tu écrivais	tu écriras
il écrit	il écrivait	il écrira
nous écrivons	nous écrivions	nous écrirons
vous écrivez	vous écriviez	vous écrirez
ils écrivent	ils écrivaient	ils écriront

PAST HISTORIC	PERFECT	PLUPERFECT
j'écrivis	j'ai écrit	j'avais écrit
tu écrivis	tu as écrit	tu avais écrit
il écrivit	il a écrit	il avait écrit
nous écrivîmes	nous avons écrit	nous avions écrit
vous écrivîtes	vous avez écrit	vous aviez écrit
ils écrivirent	ils ont écrit	ils avaient écrit

CONDITIONAL

PAST ANTERIOR	PRESENT	PAST
j'eus écrit *etc*	j'écrirais	j'aurais écrit
	tu écrirais	tu aurais écrit
	il écrirait	il aurait écrit
	nous écririons	nous aurions écrit
FUTURE PERFECT	vous écririez	vous auriez écrit
j'aurai écrit *etc*	ils écriraient	ils auraient écrit

SUBJUNCTIVE

PRESENT	IMPERFECT	PERFECT
j'écrive	j'écrivisse	j'aie écrit
tu écrives	tu écrivisses	tu aies écrit
il écrive	il écrivît	il ait écrit
nous écrivions	nous écrivissions	nous ayons écrit
vous écriviez	vous écrivissiez	vous ayez écrit
ils écrivent	ils écrivissent	ils aient écrit

IMPERATIVE / INFINITIVE / PARTICIPLE

IMPERATIVE	INFINITIVE	PARTICIPLE
écris	PRESENT	PRESENT
écrivons	écrire	écrivant
écrivez		
	PAST	PAST
	avoir écrit	écrit

VERBS

ESPÉRER *to hope*

PRESENT
j'espère
tu espères
il espère
nous espérons
vous espérez
ils espèrent

PAST HISTORIC
j'espérai
tu espéras
il espéra
nous espérâmes
vous espérâtes
ils espérèrent

IMPERFECT
j'espérais
tu espérais
il espérait
nous espérions
vous espériez
ils espéraient

PERFECT
j'ai espéré
tu as espéré
il a espéré
nous avons espéré
vous avez espéré
ils ont espéré

FUTURE
j'espérerai
tu espéreras
il espérera
nous espérerons
vous espérerez
ils espéreront

PLUPERFECT
j'avais espéré
tu avais espéré
il avait espéré
nous avions espéré
vous aviez espéré
ils avaient espéré

CONDITIONAL

PAST ANTERIOR
j'eus espéré *etc*

FUTURE PERFECT
j'aurai espéré *etc*

PRESENT
j'espérerais
tu espérerais
il espérerait
nous espérerions
vous espéreriez
ils espéreraient

PAST
j'aurais espéré
tu aurais espéré
il aurait espéré
nous aurions espéré
vous auriez espéré
ils auraient espéré

SUBJUNCTIVE

PRESENT
j'espère
tu espères
il espère
nous espérions
vous espériez
ils espèrent

IMPERFECT
j'espérasse
tu espérasses
il espérât
nous espérassions
vous espérassiez
ils espérassent

PERFECT
j'aie espéré
tu aies espéré
il ait espéré
nous ayons espéré
vous ayez espéré
ils aient espéré

IMPERATIVE

espère
espérons
espérez

INFINITIVE

PRESENT
espérer

PAST
avoir espéré

PARTICIPLE

PRESENT
espérant

PAST
espéré

ÊTRE *to be*

PRESENT	IMPERFECT	FUTURE
je suis	j'étais	je serai
tu es	tu étais	tu seras
il est	il était	il sera
nous sommes	nous étions	nous serons
vous êtes	vous étiez	vous serez
ils sont	ils étaient	ils seront

PAST HISTORIC	PERFECT	PLUPERFECT
je fus	j'ai été	j'avais été
tu fus	tu as été	tu avais été
il fut	il a été	il avait été
nous fûmes	nous avons été	nous avions été
vous fûtes	vous avez été	vous aviez été
ils furent	ils ont été	ils avaient été

CONDITIONAL

PAST ANTERIOR	PRESENT	PAST
j'eus été *etc*	je serais	j'aurais été
	tu serais	tu aurais été
	il serait	il aurait été
	nous serions	nous aurions été
FUTURE PERFECT	vous seriez	vous auriez été
j'aurai été *etc*	ils seraient	ils auraient été

SUBJUNCTIVE

PRESENT	IMPERFECT	PERFECT
je sois	je fusse	j'aie été
tu sois	tu fusses	tu aies été
il soit	il fût	il ait été
nous soyons	nous fussions	nous ayons été
vous soyez	vous fussiez	vous ayez été
ils soient	ils fussent	ils aient été

IMPERATIVE | INFINITIVE | PARTICIPLE

IMPERATIVE	INFINITIVE	PARTICIPLE
sois	PRESENT	PRESENT
soyons	être	étant
soyez		
	PAST	PAST
	avoir été	été

FAIRE *to do; to make*

PRESENT	IMPERFECT	FUTURE
je fais	je faisais	je ferai
tu fais	tu faisais	tu feras
il fait	il faisait	il fera
nous faisons	nous faisions	nous ferons
vous faites	vous faisiez	vous ferez
ils font	ils faisaient	ils feront

PAST HISTORIC	PERFECT	PLUPERFECT
je fis	j'ai fait	j'avais fait
tu fis	tu as fait	tu avais fait
il fit	il a fait	il avait fait
nous fîmes	nous avons fait	nous avions fait
vous fîtes	vous avez fait	vous aviez fait
ils firent	ils ont fait	ils avaient fait

CONDITIONAL

PAST ANTERIOR	PRESENT	PAST
j'eus fait *etc*	je ferais	j'aurais fait
	tu ferais	tu aurais fait
	il ferait	il aurait fait
	nous ferions	nous aurions fait
FUTURE PERFECT	vous feriez	vous auriez fait
j'aurai fait *etc*	ils feraient	ils auraient fait

SUBJUNCTIVE

PRESENT	IMPERFECT	PERFECT
je fasse	je fisse	j'aie fait
tu fasses	tu fisses	tu aies fait
il fasse	il fît	il ait fait
nous fassions	nous fissions	nous ayons fait
vous fassiez	vous fissiez	vous ayez fait
ils fassent	ils fissent	ils aient fait

IMPERATIVE | INFINITIVE | PARTICIPLE

IMPERATIVE	INFINITIVE	PARTICIPLE
fais	PRESENT	PRESENT
faisons	faire	faisant
faites		
	PAST	PAST
	avoir fait	fait

FALLOIR *to be necessary*

PRESENT	IMPERFECT	FUTURE
il faut	il fallait	il faudra

PAST HISTORIC	PERFECT	PLUPERFECT
il fallut	il a fallu	il avait fallu

CONDITIONAL

PAST ANTERIOR	PRESENT	PAST
il eut fallu	il faudrait	il aurait fallu

FUTURE PERFECT		
il aura fallu		

SUBJUNCTIVE

PRESENT	IMPERFECT	PERFECT
il faille	il fallût	il ait fallu

IMPERATIVE | INFINITIVE | PARTICIPLE

	PRESENT	PRESENT
	falloir	

	PAST	PAST
	avoir fallu	fallu

FINIR *to finish*

PRESENT	IMPERFECT	FUTURE
je finis	je finissais	je finirai
tu finis	tu finissais	tu finiras
il finit	il finissait	il finira
nous finissons	nous finissions	nous finirons
vous finissez	vous finissiez	vous finirez
ils finissent	ils finissaient	ils finiront

PAST HISTORIC	PERFECT	PLUPERFECT
je finis	j'ai fini	j'avais fini
tu finis	tu as fini	tu avais fini
il finit	il a fini	il avait fini
nous finîmes	nous avons fini	nous avions fini
vous finîtes	vous avez fini	vous aviez fini
ils finirent	ils ont fini	ils avaient fini

CONDITIONAL

PAST ANTERIOR	PRESENT	PAST
j'eus fini *etc*	je finirais	j'aurais fini
	tu finirais	tu aurais fini
	il finirait	il aurait fini
	nous finirions	nous aurions fini
FUTURE PERFECT	vous finiriez	vous auriez fini
j'aurai fini *etc*	ils finiraient	ils auraient fini

SUBJUNCTIVE

PRESENT	IMPERFECT	PERFECT
je finisse	je finisse	j'aie fini
tu finisses	tu finisses	tu aies fini
il finisse	il finît	il ait fini
nous finissions	nous finissions	nous ayons fini
vous finissiez	vous finissiez	vous ayez fini
ils finissent	ils finissent	ils aient fini

IMPERATIVE	INFINITIVE	PARTICIPLE
finis	PRESENT	PRESENT
finissons	finir	finissant
finissez		
	PAST	PAST
	avoir fini	fini

SE MÉFIER *to be suspicious*

PRESENT	IMPERFECT	FUTURE
je me méfie	je me méfiais	je me méfierai
tu te méfies	tu te méfiais	tu te méfieras
il se méfie	il se méfiait	il se méfiera
nous nous méfions	nous nous méfiions	nous nous méfierons
vous vous méfiez	vous vous méfiiez	vous vous méfierez
ils se méfient	ils se méfiaient	ils se méfieront

PAST HISTORIC	PERFECT	PLUPERFECT
je me méfiai	je me suis méfié(e)	je m'étais méfié(e)
tu te méfias	tu t'es méfié(e)	tu t'étais méfié(e)
il se méfia	il (elle) s'est méfié(e)	il (elle) s'était méfié(e)
nous nous méfiâmes	nous ns. sommes méfié(e)s	nous ns. étions méfié(e)s
vous vous méfiâtes	vous vs. êtes méfié(e)(s)	vous vs. étiez méfié(e)(s)
ils se méfièrent	ils (elles) se sont méfié(e)s	ils (elles) s'étaient méfié(e)s

CONDITIONAL

PAST ANTERIOR	PRESENT	PAST
je me fus méfié(e) *etc*	je me méfierais	je me serais méfié(e)
	tu te méfierais	tu te serais méfié(e)
	il se méfierait	il (elle) se serait méfié(e)
	nous ns. méfierions	nous ns. serions méfié(e)s
FUTURE PERFECT	vous vous méfieriez	vous vs. seriez méfié(e)(s)
je me serai méfié(e) *etc*	ils se méfieraient	ils (elles) se seraient méfié(e)s

SUBJUNCTIVE

PRESENT	IMPERFECT	PERFECT
je me méfie	je me méfiasse	je me sois méfié(e)
tu te méfies	tu te méfiasses	tu te sois méfié(e)
il se méfie	il se méfiât	il (elle) se soit méfié(e)
nous nous méfiions	nous nous méfiassions	nous ns. soyons méfié(e)s
vous vous méfiiez	vous vous méfiassiez	vous vs. soyez méfié(e)(s)
ils se méfient	ils se méfiassent	ils (elles) se soient méfié(e)s

IMPERATIVE	INFINITIVE	PARTICIPLE
méfie-toi	PRESENT	PRESENT
méfions-nous	se méfier	se méfiant
méfiez-vous		
	PAST	PAST
	s'être méfié(e)(s)	méfié

METTRE *to put*

PRESENT	IMPERFECT	FUTURE
je mets	je mettais	je mettrai
tu mets	tu mettais	tu mettras
il met	il mettait	il mettra
nous mettons	nous mettions	nous mettrons
vous mettez	vous mettiez	vous mettrez
ils mettent	ils mettaient	ils mettront

PAST HISTORIC	PERFECT	PLUPERFECT
je mis	j'ai mis	j'avais mis
tu mis	tu as mis	tu avais mis
il mit	il a mis	il avait mis
nous mîmes	nous avons mis	nous avions mis
vous mîtes	vous avez mis	vous aviez mis
ils mirent	ils ont mis	ils avaient mis

CONDITIONAL

PAST ANTERIOR	PRESENT	PAST
j'eus mis *etc*	je mettrais	j'aurais mis
	tu mettrais	tu aurais mis
	il mettrait	il aurait mis
	nous mettrions	nous aurions mis
FUTURE PERFECT	vous mettriez	vous auriez mis
j'aurai mis *etc*	ils mettraient	ils auraient mis

SUBJUNCTIVE

PRESENT	IMPERFECT	PERFECT
je mette	je misse	j'aie mis
tu mettes	tu misses	tu aies mis
il mette	il mît	il ait mis
nous mettions	nous missions	nous ayons mis
vous mettiez	vous missiez	vous ayez mis
ils mettent	ils missent	ils aient mis

IMPERATIVE | INFINITIVE | PARTICIPLE

IMPERATIVE	INFINITIVE	PARTICIPLE
mets	PRESENT	PRESENT
mettons	mettre	mettant
mettez		
	PAST	PAST
	avoir mis	mis

OUVRIR *to open*

PRESENT	IMPERFECT	FUTURE
j'ouvre	j'ouvrais	j'ouvrirai
tu ouvres	tu ouvrais	tu ouvriras
il ouvre	il ouvrait	il ouvrira
nous ouvrons	nous ouvrions	nous ouvrirons
vous ouvrez	vous ouvriez	vous ouvrirez
ils ouvrent	ils ouvraient	ils ouvriront

PAST HISTORIC	PERFECT	PLUPERFECT
j'ouvris	j'ai ouvert	j'avais ouvert
tu ouvris	tu as ouvert	tu avais ouvert
il ouvrit	il a ouvert	il avait ouvert
nous ouvrîmes	nous avons ouvert	nous avions ouvert
vous ouvrîtes	vous avez ouvert	vous aviez ouvert
ils ouvrirent	ils ont ouvert	ils avaient ouvert

CONDITIONAL

PAST ANTERIOR	PRESENT	PAST
j'eus ouvert *etc*	j'ouvrirais	j'aurais ouvert
	tu ouvrirais	tu aurais ouvert
	il ouvrirait	il aurait ouvert
	nous ouvririons	nous aurions ouvert
FUTURE PERFECT	vous ouvririez	vous auriez ouvert
j'aurai ouvert *etc*	ils ouvriraient	ils auraient ouvert

SUBJUNCTIVE

PRESENT	IMPERFECT	PERFECT
j'ouvre	j'ouvrisse	j'aie ouvert
tu ouvres	tu ouvrisses	tu aies ouvert
il ouvre	il ouvrît	il ait ouvert
nous ouvrions	nous ouvrissions	nous ayons ouvert
vous ouvriez	vous ouvrissiez	vous ayez ouvert
ils ouvrent	ils ouvrissent	ils aient ouvert

IMPERATIVE	INFINITIVE	PARTICIPLE
ouvre	PRESENT	PRESENT
ouvrons	ouvrir	ouvrant
ouvrez		
	PAST	PAST
	avoir ouvert	ouvert

POUVOIR *to be able to*

PRESENT	IMPERFECT	FUTURE
je peux	je pouvais	je pourrai
tu peux	tu pouvais	tu pourras
il peut	il pouvait	il pourra
nous pouvons	nous pouvions	nous pourrons
vous pouvez	vous pouviez	vous pourrez
ils peuvent	ils pouvaient	ils pourront

PAST HISTORIC	PERFECT	PLUPERFECT
je pus	j'ai pu	j'avais pu
tu pus	tu as pu	tu avais pu
il put	il a pu	il avait pu
nous pûmes	nous avons pu	nous avions pu
vous pûtes	vous avez pu	vous aviez pu
ils purent	ils ont pu	ils avaient pu

CONDITIONAL

PAST ANTERIOR	PRESENT	PAST
j'eus pu *etc*	je pourrais	j'aurais pu
	tu pourrais	tu aurais pu
	il pourrait	il aurait pu
	nous pourrions	nous aurions pu
FUTURE PERFECT	vous pourriez	vous auriez pu
j'aurai pu *etc*	ils pourraient	ils auraient pu

SUBJUNCTIVE

PRESENT	IMPERFECT	PERFECT
je puisse	je pusse	j'aie pu
tu puisses	tu pusses	tu aies pu
il puisse	il pût	il ait pu
nous puissions	nous pussions	nous ayons pu
vous puissiez	vous pussiez	vous ayez pu
ils puissent	ils pussent	ils aient pu

IMPERATIVE	INFINITIVE	PARTICIPLE
	PRESENT	PRESENT
	pouvoir	pouvant
	PAST	PAST
	avoir pu	pu

PRENDRE *to take*

PRESENT	IMPERFECT	FUTURE
je prends	je prenais	je prendrai
tu prends	tu prenais	tu prendras
il prend	il prenait	il prendra
nous prenons	nous prenions	nous prendrons
vous prenez	vous preniez	vous prendrez
ils prennent	ils prenaient	ils prendront

PAST HISTORIC	PERFECT	PLUPERFECT
je pris	j'ai pris	j'avais pris
tu pris	tu as pris	tu avais pris
il prit	il a pris	il avait pris
nous prîmes	nous avons pris	nous avions pris
vous prîtes	vous avez pris	vous aviez pris
ils prirent	ils ont pris	ils avaient pris

CONDITIONAL

PAST ANTERIOR	PRESENT	PAST
j'eus pris *etc*	je prendrais	j'aurais pris
	tu prendrais	tu aurais pris
	il prendrait	il aurait pris
	nous prendrions	nous aurions pris
FUTURE PERFECT	vous prendriez	vous auriez pris
j'aurai pris *etc*	ils prendraient	ils auraient pris

SUBJUNCTIVE

PRESENT	IMPERFECT	PERFECT
je prenne	je prisse	j'aie pris
tu prennes	tu prisses	tu aies pris
il prenne	il prît	il ait pris
nous prenions	nous prissions	nous ayons pris
vous preniez	vous prissiez	vous ayez pris
ils prennent	ils prissent	ils aient pris

IMPERATIVE	INFINITIVE	PARTICIPLE
prends	PRESENT	PRESENT
prenons	prendre	prenant
prenez		
	PAST	PAST
	avoir pris	pris

RECEVOIR *to receive*

PRESENT	IMPERFECT	FUTURE
je reçois	je recevais	je recevrai
tu reçois	tu recevais	tu recevras
il reçoit	il recevait	il recevra
nous recevons	nous recevions	nous recevrons
vous recevez	vous receviez	vous recevrez
ils reçoivent	ils recevaient	ils recevront

PAST HISTORIC	PERFECT	PLUPERFECT
je reçus	j'ai reçu	j'avais reçu
tu reçus	tu as reçu	tu avais reçu
il reçut	il a reçu	il avait reçu
nous reçûmes	nous avons reçu	nous avions reçu
vous reçûtes	vous avez reçu	vous aviez reçu
ils reçurent	ils ont reçu	ils avaient reçu

CONDITIONAL

PAST ANTERIOR	PRESENT	PAST
j'eus reçu *etc*	je recevrais	j'aurais reçu
	tu recevrais	tu aurais reçu
	il recevrait	il aurait reçu
	nous recevrions	nous aurions reçu
FUTURE PERFECT	vous recevriez	vous auriez reçu
j'aurai reçu *etc*	ils recevraient	ils auraient reçu

SUBJUNCTIVE

PRESENT	IMPERFECT	PERFECT
je reçoive	je reçusse	j'aie reçu
tu reçoives	tu reçusses	tu aies reçu
il reçoive	il reçût	il ait reçu
nous recevions	nous reçussions	nous ayons reçu
vous receviez	vous reçussiez	vous ayez reçu
ils reçoivent	ils reçussent	ils aient reçu

IMPERATIVE / INFINITIVE / PARTICIPLE

IMPERATIVE	INFINITIVE	PARTICIPLE
reçois	PRESENT	PRESENT
recevons	recevoir	recevant
recevez		
	PAST	PAST
	avoir reçu	reçu

SAVOIR *to know*

PRESENT	IMPERFECT	FUTURE
je sais	je savais	je saurai
tu sais	tu savais	tu sauras
il sait	il savait	il saura
nous savons	nous savions	nous saurons
vous savez	vous saviez	vous saurez
ils savent	ils savaient	ils sauront

PAST HISTORIC	PERFECT	PLUPERFECT
je sus	j'ai su	j'avais su
tu sus	tu as su	tu avais su
il sut	il a su	il avait su
nous sûmes	nous avons su	nous avions su
vous sûtes	vous avez su	vous aviez su
ils surent	ils ont su	ils avaient su

CONDITIONAL

PAST ANTERIOR	PRESENT	PAST
j'eus su *etc*	je saurais	j'aurais su
	tu saurais	tu aurais su
	il saurait	il aurait su
	nous saurions	nous aurions su
FUTURE PERFECT	vous sauriez	vous auriez su
j'aurai su *etc*	ils sauraient	ils auraient su

SUBJUNCTIVE

PRESENT	IMPERFECT	PERFECT
je sache	je susse	j'aie su
tu saches	tu susses	tu aies su
il sache	il sût	il ait su
nous sachions	nous sussions	nous ayons su
vous sachiez	vous sussiez	vous ayez su
ils sachent	ils sussent	ils aient su

IMPERATIVE	INFINITIVE	PARTICIPLE
sache	PRESENT	PRESENT
sachons	savoir	sachant
sachez		
	PAST	PAST
	avoir su	su

TENIR *to hold*

PRESENT	IMPERFECT	FUTURE
je tiens	je tenais	je tiendrai
tu tiens	tu tenais	tu tiendras
il tient	il tenait	il tiendra
nous tenons	nous tenions	nous tiendrons
vous tenez	vous teniez	vous tiendrez
ils tiennent	ils tenaient	ils tiendront

PAST HISTORIC	PERFECT	PLUPERFECT
je tins	j'ai tenu	j'avais tenu
tu tins	tu as tenu	tu avais tenu
il tint	il a tenu	il avait tenu
nous tînmes	nous avons tenu	nous avions tenu
vous tîntes	vous avez tenu	vous aviez tenu
ils tinrent	ils ont tenu	ils avaient tenu

CONDITIONAL

PAST ANTERIOR	PRESENT	PAST
j'eus tenu *etc*	je tiendrais	j'aurais tenu
	tu tiendrais	tu aurais tenu
	il tiendrait	il aurait tenu
	nous tiendrions	nous aurions tenu
FUTURE PERFECT	vous tiendriez	vous auriez tenu
j'aurai tenu *etc*	ils tiendraient	ils auraient tenu

SUBJUNCTIVE

PRESENT	IMPERFECT	PERFECT
je tienne	je tinsse	j'aie tenu
tu tiennes	tu tinsses	tu aies tenu
il tienne	il tînt	il ait tenu
nous tenions	nous tinssions	nous ayons tenu
vous teniez	vous tinssiez	vous ayez tenu
ils tiennent	ils tinssent	ils aient tenu

IMPERATIVE / INFINITIVE / PARTICIPLE

IMPERATIVE	INFINITIVE	PARTICIPLE
tiens	PRESENT	PRESENT
tenons	tenir	tenant
tenez		
	PAST	PAST
	avoir tenu	tenu

VENDRE *to sell*

PRESENT	IMPERFECT	FUTURE
je vends	je vendais	je vendrai
tu vends	tu vendais	tu vendras
il vend	il vendait	il vendra
nous vendons	nous vendions	nous vendrons
vous vendez	vous vendiez	vous vendrez
ils vendent	ils vendaient	ils vendront

PAST HISTORIC	PERFECT	PLUPERFECT
je vendis	j'ai vendu	j'avais vendu
tu vendis	tu as vendu	tu avais vendu
il vendit	il a vendu	il avait vendu
nous vendîmes	nous avons vendu	nous avions vendu
vous vendîtes	vous avez vendu	vous aviez vendu
ils vendirent	ils ont vendu	ils avaient vendu

CONDITIONAL

PAST ANTERIOR	PRESENT	PAST
j'eus vendu *etc*	je vendrais	j'aurais vendu
	tu vendrais	tu aurais vendu
	il vendrait	il aurait vendu
	nous vendrions	nous aurions vendu
FUTURE PERFECT	vous vendriez	vous auriez vendu
j'aurai vendu *etc*	ils vendraient	ils auraient vendu

SUBJUNCTIVE

PRESENT	IMPERFECT	PERFECT
je vende	je vendisse	j'aie vendu
tu vendes	tu vendisses	tu aies vendu
il vende	il vendît	il ait vendu
nous vendions	nous vendissions	nous ayons vendu
vous vendiez	vous vendissiez	vous ayez vendu
ils vendent	ils vendissent	ils aient vendu

IMPERATIVE	*INFINITIVE*	*PARTICIPLE*
vends	PRESENT	PRESENT
vendons	vendre	vendant
vendez		
	PAST	PAST
	avoir vendu	vendu

VENIR *to come*

PRESENT	IMPERFECT	FUTURE
je viens	je venais	je viendrai
tu viens	tu venais	tu viendras
il vient	il venait	il viendra
nous venons	nous venions	nous viendrons
vous venez	vous veniez	vous viendrez
ils viennent	ils venaient	ils viendront

PAST HISTORIC	PERFECT	PLUPERFECT
je vins	je suis venu(e)	j'étais venu(e)
tu vins	tu es venu(e)	tu étais venu(e)
il vint	il (elle) est venu(e)	il (elle) était venu(e)
nous vînmes	nous sommes venu(e)s	nous étions venu(e)s
vous vîntes	vous êtes venu(e)(s)	vous étiez venu(e)(s)
ils vinrent	ils (elles) sont venu(e)s	ils (elles) étaient venu(e)s

CONDITIONAL

	PRESENT	PAST
PAST ANTERIOR	je viendrais	je serais venu(e)
je fus venu(e) *etc*	tu viendrais	tu serais venu(e)
	il viendrait	il (elle) serait venu(e)
	nous viendrions	nous serions venu(e)s
FUTURE PERFECT	vous viendriez	vous seriez venu(e)(s)
je serai venu(e) *etc*	ils viendraient	ils (elles) seraient venu(e)s

SUBJUNCTIVE

PRESENT	IMPERFECT	PERFECT
je vienne	je vinsse	je sois venu(e)
tu viennes	tu vinsses	tu sois venu(e)
il vienne	il vînt	il (elle) soit venu(e)
nous venions	nous vinssions	nous soyons venu(e)s
vous veniez	vous vinssiez	vous soyez venu(e)(s)
ils viennent	ils vinssent	ils (elles) soient venu(e)s

IMPERATIVE	*INFINITIVE*	*PARTICIPLE*
viens	PRESENT	PRESENT
venons	venir	venant
venez		
	PAST	PAST
	être venu(e)(s)	venu

VIVRE *to live*

PRESENT	IMPERFECT	FUTURE
je vis	je vivais	je vivrai
tu vis	tu vivais	tu vivras
il vit	il vivait	il vivra
nous vivons	nous vivions	nous vivrons
vous vivez	vous viviez	vous vivrez
ils vivent	ils vivaient	ils vivront

PAST HISTORIC	PERFECT	PLUPERFECT
je vécus	j'ai vécu	j'avais vécu
tu vécus	tu as vécu	tu avais vécu
il vécut	il a vécu	il avait vécu
nous vécûmes	nous avons vécu	nous avions vécu
vous vécûtes	vous avez vécu	vous aviez vécu
ils vécurent	ils ont vécu	ils avaient vécu

CONDITIONAL

PAST ANTERIOR	PRESENT	PAST
j'eus vécu *etc*	je vivrais	j'aurais vécu
	tu vivrais	tu aurais vécu
	il vivrait	il aurait vécu
	nous vivrions	nous aurions vécu
FUTURE PERFECT	vous vivriez	vous auriez vécu
j'aurai vécu *etc*	ils vivraient	ils auraient vécu

SUBJUNCTIVE

PRESENT	IMPERFECT	PERFECT
je vive	je vécusse	j'aie vécu
tu vives	tu vécusses	tu aies vécu
il vive	il vécût	il ait vécu
nous vivions	nous vécussions	nous ayons vécu
vous viviez	vous vécussiez	vous ayez vécu
ils vivent	ils vécussent	ils aient vécu

IMPERATIVE | INFINITIVE | PARTICIPLE

IMPERATIVE	INFINITIVE	PARTICIPLE
vis	**PRESENT**	**PRESENT**
vivons	vivre	vivant
vivez		
	PAST	**PAST**
	avoir vécu	vécu

VOIR *to see*

PRESENT	**IMPERFECT**	**FUTURE**
je vois	je voyais	je verrai
tu vois	tu voyais	tu verras
il voit	il voyait	il verra
nous voyons	nous voyions	nous verrons
vous voyez	vous voyiez	vous verrez
ils voient	ils voyaient	ils verront

PAST HISTORIC	**PERFECT**	**PLUPERFECT**
je vis	j'ai vu	j'avais vu
tu vis	tu as vu	tu avais vu
il vit	il a vu	il avait vu
nous vîmes	nous avons vu	nous avions vu
vous vîtes	vous avez vu	vous aviez vu
ils virent	ils ont vu	ils avaient vu

CONDITIONAL

PAST ANTERIOR	**PRESENT**	**PAST**
j'eus vu *etc*	je verrais	j'aurais vu
	tu verrais	tu aurais vu
	il verrait	il aurait vu
	nous verrions	nous aurions vu
FUTURE PERFECT	vous verriez	vous auriez vu
j'aurai vu *etc*	ils verraient	ils auraient vu

SUBJUNCTIVE

PRESENT	**IMPERFECT**	**PERFECT**
je voie	je visse	j'aie vu
tu voies	tu visses	tu aies vu
il voie	il vît	il ait vu
nous voyions	nous vissions	nous ayons vu
vous voyiez	vous vissiez	vous ayez vu
ils voient	ils vissent	ils aient vu

IMPERATIVE | INFINITIVE | PARTICIPLE

IMPERATIVE	**INFINITIVE**	**PARTICIPLE**
vois	**PRESENT**	**PRESENT**
voyons	voir	voyant
voyez		
	PAST	**PAST**
	avoir vu	vu

VOULOIR *to want*

PRESENT	IMPERFECT	FUTURE
je veux	je voulais	je voudrai
tu veux	tu voulais	tu voudras
il veut	il voulait	il voudra
nous voulons	nous voulions	nous voudrons
vous voulez	vous vouliez	vous voudrez
ils veulent	ils voulaient	ils voudront

PAST HISTORIC	PERFECT	PLUPERFECT
je voulus	j'ai voulu	j'avais voulu
tu voulus	tu as voulu	tu avais voulu
il voulut	il a voulu	il avait voulu
nous voulûmes	nous avons voulu	nous avions voulu
vous voulûtes	vous avez voulu	vous aviez voulu
ils voulurent	ils ont voulu	ils avaient voulu

CONDITIONAL

PAST ANTERIOR	PRESENT	PAST
j'eus voulu *etc*	je voudrais	j'aurais voulu
	tu voudrais	tu aurais voulu
	il voudrait	il aurait voulu
	nous voudrions	nous aurions voulu
FUTURE PERFECT	vous voudriez	vous auriez voulu
j'aurai voulu *etc*	ils voudraient	ils auraient voulu

SUBJUNCTIVE

PRESENT	IMPERFECT	PERFECT
je veuille	je voulusse	j'aie voulu
tu veuilles	tu voulusses	tu aies voulu
il veuille	il voulût	il ait voulu
nous voulions	nous voulussions	nous ayons voulu
vous vouliez	vous voulussiez	vous ayez voulu
ils veuillent	ils voulussent	ils aient voulu

IMPERATIVE

IMPERATIVE	INFINITIVE	PARTICIPLE
veuille	PRESENT	PRESENT
veuillons	vouloir	voulant
veuillez		
	PAST	PAST
	avoir voulu	voulu

M VERBAL CONSTRUCTIONS

There are two main types of verbal construction:

1 Verbs followed by an infinitive

There are three main types of construction when a verb is followed by an infinitive. For examples of all three types, see **pp 142-50.**

a) *Verbs followed by an infinitive without any linking preposition*

These include verbs of wishing and willing, of movement and of perception:

adorer	to love
aimer	to like
aimer mieux	to prefer
aller	to go (and)
compter	to intend to
descendre	to go down (and)
désirer	to wish
détester	to hate
devoir	to have to
écouter	to listen to
entendre	to hear
entrer	to go in (and)
envoyer	to send
espérer	to hope to
faire	to make
falloir	to have to
laisser	to let
monter	to go up (and)
oser	to dare
pouvoir	to be able to
préférer	to prefer to

regarder	to watch
rentrer	to go in/back (and)
savoir	to know how to
sembler	to seem
sentir	to feel
sortir	to go out (and)
souhaiter	to wish to
valoir mieux	to be better to
venir	to come (and)
voir	to see
vouloir	to want to

b) *Verbs followed by* à + infinitive

aider à	to help (to do)
s'amuser à	to enjoy (doing)
apprendre à	to learn (to do)
s'apprêter à	to get ready (to do)
arriver à	to manage (to do)
s'attendre à	to expect (to do)
autoriser à	to allow (to do)
chercher à	to try (to do)
commencer à	to start (doing)
consentir à	to agree (to do)
consister à	to consist in (doing)
continuer à	to continue (to do)
se décider à	to make up one's mind (to do)
encourager à	to encourage (to do)
enseigner à	to teach how (to do)
forcer à	to force (to do)
s'habituer à	to get used (to doing)
hésiter à	to hesitate (to do)
inciter à	to prompt (to do)
s'intéresser à	to be interested in (doing)

inviter à	to invite (to do)
se mettre à	to start (doing)
obliger à	to force (to do)
parvenir à	to succeed (in doing)
passer son temps à	to spend one's time (doing)
perdre son temps à	to waste one's time (doing)
persister à	to persist in (doing)
pousser à	to urge (to do)
se préparer à	to get ready (to do)
renoncer à	to give up (doing)
rester à	to be left (to do)
réussir à	to manage (to do)
servir à	to be used for (doing)
songer à	to think of (doing)
tarder à	to delay/be late in (doing)
tenir à	to be keen (to do)

c) *Verbs followed by* de + infinitive:

accepter de	to agree (to do)
accuser de	to accuse of (doing)
achever de	to finish (doing)
s'arrêter de	to stop (doing)
avoir besoin de	to need (to do)
avoir envie de	to feel like (doing)
avoir peur de	to be afraid (to do)
cesser de	to stop (doing)
se charger de	to undertake (to do)
commander de	to order (to do)
conseiller de	to advise (to do)
se contenter de	to make do with (doing)
craindre de	to be afraid (to do)
décider de	to decide (to do)
déconseiller de	to advise against (doing)

défendre de	to forbid (to do)
demander de	to ask (to do)
se dépêcher de	to hasten (to do)
dire de	to tell (to do)
dissuader de	to dissuade from (doing)
s'efforcer de	to strive (to do)
empêcher de	to prevent (from doing)
s'empresser de	to hasten (to do)
entreprendre de	to undertake (to do)
essayer de	to try (to do)
s'étonner de	to be surprised (at doing)
éviter de	to avoid (doing)
s'excuser de	to apologize for (doing)
faire semblant de	to pretend (to do)
feindre de	to pretend (to do)
finir de	to finish (doing)
se garder de	to be careful not to (do)
se hâter de	to hasten (to do)
interdire de	to forbid (to do)
jurer de	to swear (to do)
manquer de	'to nearly' (do)
menacer de	to threaten (to do)
mériter de	to deserve (to do)
négliger de	to fail (to do)
s'occuper de	to undertake (to do)
offrir de	to offer (to do)
omettre de	to omit (to do)
ordonner de	to order (to do)
oublier de	to forget (to do)
permettre de	to allow (to do)
persuader de	to persuade (to do)
prier de	to ask (to do)
promettre de	to promise (to do)
proposer de	to offer (to do)

recommander de	to recommend (to do)
refuser de	to refuse (to do)
regretter de	to be sorry (to do)
remercier de	to thank for (doing)
résoudre de	to resolve (to do)
risquer de	to risk (doing)
se souvenir de	to remember (doing)
suggérer de	to suggest (doing)
supplier de	to implore (to do)
tâcher de	to try (to do)
tenter de	to try (to do)
venir de	to have just (done)

2 Verbs followed by an object

In general, verbs which take a direct object in French also take a direct object in English, and verbs which take an indirect object in French (ie verb + preposition + object) also take an indirect object in English.

There are, however, some exceptions:

a) *Verbs followed by an indirect object in English but not in French* (the English preposition is not translated):

attendre	to wait for
chercher	to look for
demander	to ask for
écouter	to listen to
espérer	to hope for
payer	to pay for
regarder	to look at
reprocher	to blame for

on a demandé l'addition
we asked for the bill

j'attendais l'autobus
I was waiting for the bus

je cherche mon frère
I'm looking for my brother

tu écoutes la radio?
are you listening to the radio?

b) *Verbs which take a direct object in English, but an indirect object in French:*

convenir à	to suit
se fier à	to trust
jouer à	to play *(game, sport)*
jouer de	to play *(musical instrument)*
obéir à	to obey
désobéir à	to disobey
pardonner à	to forgive
renoncer à	to give up
répondre à	to answer
résister à	to resist
ressembler à	to resemble (to look like)
téléphoner à	to phone

tu peux te fier à moi
you can trust me

tu joues souvent au tennis?
do you often play tennis?

il joue bien de la guitare
he plays the guitar well

tu as répondu à ma lettre?
did you answer my letter?

téléphonons au médecin
let's phone the doctor

obéis à ton père!
obey your father!

c) *Verbs which take a direct object in English but* de + *indirect object in French:*

s'apercevoir de	to notice
s'approcher de	to come near
avoir besoin de	to need
changer de	to change
douter de	to doubt
se douter de	to suspect
s'emparer de	to seize, to grab
jouir de	to enjoy
manquer de	to lack, to miss

se méfier de	to mistrust
se servir de	to use
se souvenir de	to remember
se tromper de ...	to get the wrong ...

je dois changer de train?
do I have to change trains?

il ne s'est aperçu de rien
he didn't notice anything

méfiez-vous de lui
don't trust him

je me servirai de ton vélo
I'll use your bike

tu te souviens de Jean?
do you remember Jean?

il s'est trompé de numéro
he got the wrong number

d) *Some verbs take* à *or* de *before an object, whereas their English equivalent uses a different preposition:*

i) Verb + à + object:

croire à	to believe in
s'intéresser à	to be interested in
penser à	to think of/about
songer à	to think of
rêver à	to dream of/about
servir à	to be used for

je m'intéresse au football et à la course automobile
I'm interested in football and in motor-racing

à quoi penses-tu?
what are you thinking about?

ça sert à quoi?
what is it (used) for?

ii) Verb + de + object:

dépendre de	to depend on
être fâché de	to be annoyed at
féliciter de	to congratulate for
parler de	to speak of/about
remercier de	to thank for
rire de	to laugh at
traiter de	to deal with, to be about
vivre de	to live on

cela dépendra du temps	**il m'a parlé de toi**
it'll depend on the weather	he told me about you

tu l'as remercié du cadeau qu'il t'a fait?
did you thank him for the present he gave you?

3 Verbs followed by one direct object and one indirect object

a) In general, these are verbs of giving or lending, and their English equivalents are constructed in the same way, eg:

donner quelque chose à quelqu'un
to give something to someone

il a vendu son ordinateur à son voisin
he sold his computer to his neighbour

Note that after such verbs, the preposition 'to' is often omitted in English but à, however, cannot be omitted in French. Particular care must be taken when object pronouns are used with these verbs (*see* pp 78-9).

b) With verbs expressing 'taking away', à is translated by 'from' (qn stands for 'quelqu'un' and sb for 'somebody'):

acheter à qn	to buy from sb
cacher à qn	to hide from sb
demander à qn	to ask sb for
emprunter à qn	to borrow from sb
enlever à qn	to take away from sb
ôter à qn	to take away from sb
prendre à qn	to take from sb
voler à qn	to steal from sb

à qui as-tu emprunté cela?	**il l'a volé à son frère**
who did you borrow this from?	he stole it from his brother

4 Verb + indirect object + de + infinitive

Some verbs which take a direct object in English are followed by
à + object + de + infinitive in French:

commander à qn de faire	to order sb to do
conseiller à qn de faire	to advise sb to do
défendre à qn de faire	to forbid sb to do
demander à qn de faire	to ask sb to do
dire à qn de faire	to tell sb to do
ordonner à qn de faire	to order sb to do
permettre à qn de faire	to allow sb to do
promettre à qn de faire	to promise sb to do
proposer à qn de faire	to offer to do for sb, to suggest to sb to do

je leur ai conseillé de ne pas essayer
I advised them not to try

demande à ton fils de t'aider
ask your son to help you

j'ai promis à mes parents de ne jamais recommencer
I promised my parents never to do this again

8 PREPOSITIONS

Prepositions in both French and English can have many different meanings, which presents considerable difficulties for the translator. The following guide to the most common prepositions sets out the generally accepted meanings on the left, with a description of their use in brackets, and an illustration. The main meanings are given first. Prepositions are listed in alphabetical order.

À

AT	(place)	**au troisième arrêt**
		at the third stop
	(date)	**à Noël**
		at Christmas
	(time)	**à trois heures**
		at three o'clock
	(idioms)	**au hasard**
		at random
		au travail
		at work
IN	(place)	**à Montmartre**
		in Montmartre
		à Lyon
		in Lyons
		au supermarché
		in the supermarket
		à la campagne
		in the country
		au lit
		in bed
		au loin
		in the distance

	(manner)	**à la française**
		in the French way
		à ma façon
		my way
TO	*(place)*	**aller au théâtre**
		to go to the theatre
		aller à Londres
		to go to London
	*(+ infinitive)**	**c'est facile à faire**
		it is easy to do (*see* p 147)
AWAY FROM	*(distance)*	**à 3 km d'ici**
		3 km away
BY	*(means)*	**aller à vélo**
		to go by bike
		je l'ai reconnu à ses habits
		I recognized him by his clothing
	(manner)	**fait à la main**
		hand-made
	(rate)	**à la centaine**
		by the hundred
		100 km à l'heure
		100 km per hour
FOR/UP TO	*(+ pronoun)*	**c'est à vous de jouer**
		it's your turn
		c'est à nous de te le dire
		it's up to us to tell you
	(purpose)	**une tasse à café**
		a coffee cup
FROM		**il l'a caché à ses parents**
		he hid it from his parents
HIS/HER/MY	*(possessive)*	**son sac à elle**
ETC		her bag
ON	*(means)*	**aller à cheval/à pied**
		to go on horseback/on foot

	(place)	**à la page 12**
		on page 12
		à droite/à gauche
		on/to the right/left
	(time)	**à cette occasion**
		on this occasion
WITH	*(descriptive)*	**un homme aux cheveux blonds**
		a man with blond hair
		l'homme à la valise
		the man with the suitcase
	(idiom)	**à bras ouverts**
		with open arms

For use of the preposition à with the infinitive see Verbal Constructions, pp 197–8.

APRÈS

AFTER	*(time)*	**après votre arrivée**
		after your arrival
	(sequence)	**24 ans après la mort du président**
		24 years after the death of the President
		je suis allé au lit après avoir fini le livre
		I went to bed after I finished the book
		après s'être séparée de son mari
		after separating from her husband

AUPRÈS DE

BESIDE		**il s'assit auprès de sa mère**
		he sat down beside his mother
COMPARED TO		**ce n'est rien auprès de ce que tu as fait**
		it's nothing compared to what you've done

AVANT

BEFORE	*(time)*	**avant cet après-midi**
		before this afternoon
		avant ce soir
		before tonight
		avant de s'asseoir
		before sitting down
	(preference)	**la famille avant tout**
		the family comes first (above all else)

AVEC

WITH	*(association)*	**je viendrai avec lui**
		I'll come with him
	(means)	**elle marche avec une canne**
		she walks with a stick

CHEZ

AT	*(place)*	**chez moi/toi**
		at/to my/your house
		chez mon oncle
		at my uncle's
		chez le pharmacien
		at the chemist's
AMONG		**chez les Écossais**
		among the Scots
ABOUT		**ce qui m'énerve chez toi, c'est ...**
		what annoys me about you is ...
IN		**chez Sartre**
		in Sartre's work

CONTRE

AGAINST	*(place)*	**contre le mur**
		against the wall
WITH	*(after verb)*	**je suis fâché contre elle**
		I'm angry with her
FOR		**elle a échangé un billet contre des pièces**
		she changed a note for coins

DANS

IN	*(position)*	**dans ma serviette**
		in my briefcase
	(time)	**je pars dans deux jours**
		I'm leaving in two days' time
	(idiom)	**dans l'attente de vous voir**
		looking forward to seeing you
FROM	*(removal)*	**prendre quelque chose dans l'armoire**
		to take something from the cupboard
ON	*(position)*	**dans le train**
		on the train
OUT OF	*(idiom)*	**boire dans un verre**
		to drink out of a glass

DE

FROM	*(place)*	**je suis venu de Glasgow**
		I have come from Glasgow
	(date)	**du 5 février au 10 mars**
		from 5 February to 10 March
		d'un week-end à l'autre
		from one weekend to another
OF	*(adjectival)*	**un cri de triomphe**
		a shout of triumph
	(contents)	**une tasse de café**
		a cup of coffee
	(cause)	**mourir de faim**
		to die of hunger
	(measurement)	**long de 3 mètres**
		3 metres long
	(time)	**ma montre retarde de 10 minutes**
		my watch is 10 minutes slow
	(price)	**le montant est de 20 euros**
		the total is 20 euros
	(possessive)	**le père de mon ami**
		my friend's father
	(adjectival)	**les vacances de Pâques**
		the Easter holidays

	(after 'quelque chose')	**quelque chose de bon** something good
	(after 'rien')	**rien de nouveau** nothing new
	(after 'personne')	**personne d'autre** nobody else
	(quantity)	**beaucoup de, peu de** many, few
BY	*(idiom)*	**je le connais de vue** I know him by sight
IN	*(manner)*	**de cette façon** in this way
	(after superlatives)	**la plus haute montagne d'Écosse** the highest mountain in Scotland
ON	*(position)*	**de ce côté** on this side
THAN	*(comparative)*	**moins de 2 euros** less than 2 euros **plus de 3 litres** more than 3 litres
TO	*(after adjectives)*	**ravi de vous voir** delighted to see you **il est facile de se tromper** it is easy to make a mistake
	(after verbs)	**s'efforcer de** to try to
WITH	*(cause)*	**tomber de fatigue** to drop with exhaustion
DEPUIS		
FOR	*(time)*	**j'étudie le français depuis 3 ans** I have been studying French for 3 years **j'étudiais le français depuis 3 ans** I had been studying French for 3 years **je n'y ai pas joué depuis des années** I haven't played for years

FROM	*(place)*	**depuis ma fenêtre, je vois la mer**
		from my window I can see the sea
	(time)	**depuis le matin jusqu'au soir**
		from morning till evening
SINCE		**depuis Dimanche**
		since Sunday

DERRIÈRE

| BEHIND | *(place)* | **derrière la maison** |
| | | behind the house |

DÈS

FROM	*(time)*	**dès six heures**
		from six o'clock onwards
		dès 1934
		as far back as 1934
		dès le début
		from the beginning
		dès maintenant
		from now on
	(place)	**dès Édimbourg**
		from (the moment of leaving) Edinburgh

DEVANT

IN FRONT OF	*(place)*	**devant l'école**
		in front of the school
BEFORE	*(place)*	**sur la table devant eux**
		on the table before them

EN

IN	*(place)*	**être en ville**
		to be in town
		en Angleterre
		in England
	(colour)	**un mur peint en jaune**
		a wall painted yellow

	(material)	**une montre en or**
		a gold watch
BY	(means)	**en auto/en avion**
		by car/by plane
	(dates, seasons)	**en quelle année?**
		in what year?
		en 2002
		in 2002
		en été
		in the summer
		en juillet
		in July
	(dress)	**en jupe**
		in a skirt
	(language)	**en chinois**
		in Chinese
	(time)	**j'ai fait mes devoirs en 20 minutes**
		I did my homework in 20 minutes
LIKE, AS		**il s'est habillé en femme**
		he dressed as a woman
ON	(idiom)	**en vacances**
		on holiday
		en moyenne
		on average
	(+ present participle)	**en faisant**
		on/while/by doing

Note that en is not used with the definite article except in certain expressions: en l'an 2020 *(in the year 2020),* en l'honneur de *(in honour of) and* en la présence de *(in the presence of).*

EN TANT QUE

AS/IN ONE'S CAPACITY AS	**en tant que professeur**
	as a teacher

ENTRE

AMONG		**être entre amis**
		to be among friends
BETWEEN	*(place)*	**entre Londres et Paris**
		between London and Paris
	(time)	**entre 6 et 10 heures**
		between 6 and 10 o'clock
	(idiom)	**entre nous**
		between you and me
IN	*(punctuation)*	**entre guillemets**
		in inverted commas
		entre parenthèses
		in brackets

D'ENTRE

OF/FROM AMONG   **certains d'entre eux**
some of them

ENVERS

TO/TOWARDS   **être bien disposé envers quelqu'un**
to be well-disposed towards someone

HORS DE

OUT OF   **hors de danger**
out of danger

JUSQUE

UP TO/	*(place)*	**jusqu'à la frontière espagnole**
AS FAR AS		as far as the Spanish border
	(time)	**jusqu'ici**
		up to now
		jusque-là
		up till then
TILL		**jusqu'à demain**
		till tomorrow

MALGRÉ

IN SPITE OF   **malgré la chaleur**
in spite of the heat

PAR

BY	*(agent)*	**la décision fut prise par le président**
		the decision was made by the President
	(means of transport)	**par le train**
		by train
	(distributive)	**trois fois par semaine**
		three times a week
		deux par deux
		two by two
	(place)	**par ici/là**
		this/that way
IN/ON	*(weather)*	**par un temps pareil**
		in such weather
		par un beau jour d'hiver
		on a beautiful winter's day
THROUGH/ OUT OF	*(place)*	**regarder par la fenêtre**
		to look out of the window
		jette-le par la fenêtre
		throw it out of the window
TO/ON		**tomber par terre**
		to fall to the ground
		étendu par terre
		lying on the ground
	(+ infinitive)	**commencer/finir par faire**
		to begin/end by doing

PARMI

| AMONG | | **parmi mes ennemis** |
| | | among my enemies |

PENDANT

FOR	*(time)*	**il l'avait fait pendant 5 ans**
		he had done it for 5 years
DURING		**pendant l'été**
		during the summer

POUR

FOR		ce livre est pour vous
		this book is for you
		mourir pour la patrie
		to die for one's country
	(purpose)	c'est pour cela que je suis venu
		that's why I've come
	(emphatic)	pour moi, cet argument ne tient pas
		if you ask me, this argument isn't valid
	*(time)**	j'en ai pour une heure
		it'll take me an hour
		je suis en vacances pour 2 semaines
		I'm on holiday for 2 weeks
	(idiom)	c'est bon pour la santé
		it's good for your health
TO	*(+ infinitive)*	il était trop paresseux pour réussir ses examens
		he was too lazy to pass his exams

*(pour *stresses intention and future time: see* depuis *and* pendant, pp 210, 214)

PRÈS

NEAR	*(place)*	près du marché
		near the market
NEARLY	*(time)*	il est près de minuit
		it's nearly midnight
	(quantity)	près de cinquante
		nearly fifty

QUANT À

AS FOR		quant à moi
		as for me

SANS

WITHOUT	*(+ noun)*	sans espoir
		without hope
	(+ pronoun)	je n'irai pas sans vous
		I won't go without you

	(+ infinitive)	**sans parler** without speaking **sans s'arrêter** without stopping

SAUF

EXCEPT FOR		**ils sont tous partis, sauf Jean** everyone left except Jean
BARRING		**sauf accidents/sauf imprévu** barring accidents/the unexpected

SELON

ACCORDING TO		**selon le président** according to the President **selon moi** in my opinion

SOUS

UNDER	*(physical)*	**sous la table** under the table
	(governed by)	**sous Élisabeth II** under Elizabeth II
IN	*(weather)*	**sous la pluie** in the rain
	(idiom)	**sous peu** before long/shortly **sous la main** to hand **sous tous rapports** in all respects **sous mes yeux** before my eyes

SUR

ON/UPON	*(place)*	**le chat est sur le toit** the cat's on the roof

OFF		je l'ai pris sur l'étagère
		I took it off the shelf
OUT OF	*(proportion)*	neuf sur dix
		nine out of ten
		une semaine sur trois
		one week in three
OVER	*(place)*	le pont sur la Loire
		the bridge over the Loire
		l'emporter sur quelqu'un
		to prevail over someone
ABOUT	*(idiom)*	une enquête sur ...
		an enquiry about ...
WITH		sur ces paroles
		with these words
		sur ce, il est sorti
		with that he went out
BY		quatre mètres sur cinq
		four metres by five
IN		sur un ton amer
		in a bitter tone (of voice)

VERS

TOWARDS	*(place)*	vers le nord
		towards the north
	(time)	vers la fin du match
		towards the end of the match
ABOUT	*(time)*	vers 10 heures
		about 10 o'clock

VOICI/VOILÀ

HERE		le voici qui vient
		here he comes
THERE		voilà où il demeure
		that's where he lives

9 CONJUNCTIONS

Conjunctions are words or expressions which link words, phrases or clauses. They fall into two categories, coordinating conjunctions and subordinating conjunctions:

A COORDINATING CONJUNCTIONS

1 Definition

These link two similar words or groups of words, eg nouns, pronouns, adjectives, adverbs, prepositions, phrases or clauses. The principal coordinating conjunctions (or adverbs used as conjunctions) are:

et (and)	**mais** (but)	**ou** (or)
ou bien (or (else))	**soit** (either)	**ni** (neither)
alors (then)	**aussi** (therefore)	**donc** (then, therefore)
puis (then, next)	**car** (for, because)	**or** (now)
cependant (however)	**néanmoins** (nevertheless)	
pourtant (yet, however)	**toutefois** (however)	

il est malade mais il ne veut pas aller au lit
he's ill but he won't go to bed

il faisait beau alors il est allé se promener
it was nice weather so he went for a walk

2 Repetition

a) Some coordinating conjunctions are repeated:

soit ... soit ...   **ou (bien) ... ou (bien) ...**
either ... or ...   either ... or ...

soit tu viens avec nous, soit tu restes ici mais tu te décides
either you come with us or you stay here, but you have to decide

ou tu t'habitues ou tu démissionnes
either you get used to it or you resign

prenez soit l'un soit l'autre   **ni ... ni ...**
take one or the other   neither ... nor ...

le vieillard n'avait ni amis ni argent
the old man had neither friends nor money

b) et and ou can be repeated in texts of a literary nature:

et ... et ...   **ou ... ou ...**
both ... and ...   either ... or ...

elle ne cessa et de crier et de pleurer
she didn't stop shouting and crying

ou c'est lui ou c'est moi !
it's either him or me!

3 aussi

aussi means 'therefore' only when placed before the verb. The subject pronoun is placed after the verb (*see* **pp 238-9**).

il pleuvait, aussi Pascal n'est-il pas sorti
it was raining, so Pascal didn't go out

When aussi follows the verb it means 'also':

j'ai aussi emporté des pulls, au cas où
I also brought some jumpers, just in case

B **SUBORDINATING CONJUNCTIONS**

These join a subordinate clause to another clause, usually a main clause. The principal subordinating conjunctions are:

comme	as	parce que	because
puisque	since	ainsi que	(just) as
à mesure que	as	tant que	as long as
avant que	before	après que	after
jusqu'à ce que	until	depuis que	since
pendant que	while	tandis que	whereas
si	if	à moins que	unless
pourvu que	provided that	quoique	although
bien que	although	quand	when
lorsque	when	dès que	as soon as
aussitôt que	as soon as	pour que	in order that
afin que	so that	de sorte que	so that
de façon que	so that	de peur que (+ ne)	for fear that, lest

Note that some subordinating conjunctions require the subjunctive (*see* pp 134-5).

 C **QUE**

1 Coordinating (*see* pp 46-7; 57-9)

que is a coordinating conjunction when used in comparisons:

il est plus fort que moi
he is stronger than I

elle est plus courageuse que tu ne crois
she's braver than you think

2 Subordinating

a) *meaning 'that':*

elle dit qu'elle l'a vu
she says she has seen him

je pense que tu as raison
I think you're right

il faut que tu viennes
you'll have to come

il paraît qu'elle a gagné
it seems she's won

b) *replacing another conjunction:*

When a conjunction introduces more than one verb, que usually replaces the second subordinating conjunction and any subsequent ones to avoid repetition:

comme il était tard et que j'étais fatigué, je suis rentré
as it was late and I was tired, I went home

s'il fait beau et que tu es libre, nous irons à la piscine
if the weather's nice and you're free, we'll go to the swimming pool

nous sortirons lorsque nous aurons déjeuné et que tu te seras reposé
we'll go out when we've had lunch and you've had a rest

10 NUMBERS AND QUANTITIES

A CARDINAL NUMBERS

0	zéro	40	quarante
1	un (une)	50	cinquante
2	deux	60	soixante
3	trois	70	soixante-dix
4	quatre	71	soixante et onze
5	cinq	72	soixante-douze
6	six	80	quatre-vingt(s)
7	sept	90	quatre-vingt-dix
8	huit	99	quatre-vingt-dix-neuf
9	neuf	100	cent
10	dix	101	cent un(e)
11	onze	102	cent deux
12	douze	121	cent vingt et un(e)
13	treize	122	cent vingt-deux
14	quatorze	200	deux cents
15	quinze	201	deux cent un(e)
16	seize	1000	mille
17	dix-sept	1988	mille neuf cent
18	dix-huit		quatre-vingt-huit
19	dix-neuf	2000	deux mille
20	vingt	10,000	dix mille
30	trente	1,000,000	un million

Note

• Un is the only cardinal number which agrees with the noun in gender:

un kilo	**une pomme**
a kilo	an apple

Note—cont'd

- Hyphens are used in compound numbers between 17 and 99 except where et is used (this also applies to compound numbers after 100: cent vingt-trois = 123).

- Cent and mille are not preceded by un as in English (one hundred).

- Vingt and cent multiplied by a number take an s when they are not followed by another number.

il a quatre-vingts ans
he's eighty

elle a remporté quatre-vingt-deux victoires
she has notched up eighty-two wins

c'est une civilisation vieille de huit cents ans
it's a civilization which is eight hundred years old

ce livre compte trois cent cinq pages
this book has three hundred and five pages

- Mille is invariable.

trente mille personnes ont assisté à la rencontre
thirty thousand people went to the match

B ORDINAL NUMBERS

		abbreviation
1st	**premier/première**	1er/1ère
2nd	**deuxième/second**	2e
3rd	**troisième**	3e
4th	**quatrième**	4e
5th	**cinquième**	5e
6th	**sixième**	6e
7th	**septième**	7e
8th	**huitième**	8e

9th	neuvième	9^e
10th	dixième	10^e
11th	onzième	11^e
12th	douzième	12^e
13th	treizième	13^e
14th	quatorzième	14^e
15th	quinzième	15^e
16th	seizième	16^e
17th	dix-septième	17^e
18th	dix-huitième	18^e
19th	dix-neuvième	19^e
20th	vingtième	20^e
21st	vingt et unième	21^e
22nd	vingt-deuxième	22^e
30th	trentième	30^e
100th	centième	100^e
101st	cent unième	101^e
200th	deux centième	200^e
1000th	millième	1000^e
10,000th	dix millième	$10\ 000^e$

Note

- Ordinal numbers are formed by adding -ième to cardinal numbers, except for premier and second; cinq, neuf and numbers ending in e undergo slight changes: cinquième, neuvième, onzième, douzième etc.

- Ordinal numbers agree with the noun in gender and number:

le Premier ministre	**la première fleur du printemps**
the Prime Minister	the first flower of spring

- There is no elision with huitième and onzième:

le huitième jour	**du onzième candidat**
the eighth day	of the eleventh candidate

- Cardinal numbers are used for monarchs, except for 'first':

Charles deux	**Charles premier**
Charles II	Charles I

C FRACTIONS AND PROPORTIONS

1 Fractions

Fractions are expressed as in English: cardinal followed by ordinal:

> **deux cinquièmes**
> two fifths

But:	**¹/₄ un quart**	**¹/₂ un demi, une demie**
	¹/₃ un tiers	**³/₄ trois quarts**

2 Decimals

The English decimal point is conveyed by a comma in French:

> **un virgule huit (1,8)**
> one point eight (1.8)

3 Approximate numbers

une huitaine	**une dizaine**
about eight	about ten
une trentaine	**une centaine**
some thirty	about a hundred

But:	**un millier**
	about a thousand

Note that **de** is used when the approximate number is followed by a noun:

> **une vingtaine d'enfants**
> about twenty children

4 Arithmetic

Addition:	**deux plus quatre**	2+4
Subtraction:	**cinq moins deux**	5−2
Multiplication:	**trois fois cinq**	3×5
Division:	**six divisé par deux**	6÷2
Square:	**deux au carré**	2^2
Power:	**deux puissance six**	2^6

D MEASUREMENTS AND PRICES

1 Measurements

a) *Dimensions*

long(ue)/de longueur/de long	long
profond(e)/de profondeur/de profond	deep
épais(se)/d'épaisseur	thick
haut(e)/de hauteur/de haut	high

la salle de classe est longue de 12 mètres
la salle de classe a/fait 12 mètres de longueur/de long
the classroom is 12 metres long

ma chambre fait quatre mètres sur trois
my bedroom is about four metres by three

b) *Distance*

à quelle distance sommes-nous de la gare?
how far are we from the station?

nous sommes à deux kilomètres de la gare
we are two kilometres from the station

combien y a-t-il d'ici à Blois?
how far is it to Blois?

2 Price

ce pull m'a coûté 20 euros	j'ai payé ce pull 20 euros
this sweater cost me 20 euros	I paid 20 euros for this sweater
cela fait/revient à 6 euros	ils coûtent 4 euros pièce
that comes to 6 euros	they cost 4 euros each
du vin blanc à 3 euros la bouteille	des pommes à 2 euros le kilo
white wine at 3 euros a bottle	apples at 2 euros a kilo

E EXPRESSIONS OF QUANTITY

Quantity may be expressed by an adverb of quantity, eg 'a lot', 'too much' or by a noun which names the actual quantity involved, eg 'a bottle', 'a dozen'.

1 Expression of quantity + de + noun

Before a noun, adverbs and other expressions of quantity are followed by de (d' before a vowel or a silent h) and never by du, de la or des, except for bien des and la plupart du/des:

combien de how much/many	**assez de** enough
beaucoup de a lot of/much/many	**autant de** as much/many
moins de less/fewer	**plus de** more
peu de little/few	**un peu de** a little
tant de so much/many	**tellement de** so much/many
bien du/de la/des many/a lot of	**la plupart du/de la/des** most
trop de too much/many	

il y a assez de fromage? is there enough cheese?	**autant de gens** as many people
je n'ai pas beaucoup de temps I haven't got much time	**il y a combien de pièces?** how many rooms are there?
j'ai mis moins de temps que lui I took less time than him	**mange plus de légumes!** eat more vegetables!
peu de gens le savent not many people know that	**tu veux un peu de pain?** would you like a little bread?

il y a tant d'années
so many years ago

j'ai tellement de travail
I've got so much work

bien des gens
a good many people

la plupart des Français
most French people

tu as bien de la patience
you have a lot of patience

il y a trop de voitures
there are too many cars

2 Noun expressing quantity + de + noun

une boîte de
a box/tin/can/jar of

une bouteille de
a bottle of

une bouchée de
a mouthful of *(drink)*

une cuillerée de
a spoonful of

une douzaine de
a dozen

une gorgée de
a mouthful of *(drink)*

un kilo de
a kilo of

un litre de
a litre of

une livre de
a pound of

un morceau de
a piece of

un paquet de
a packet of

une paire de
a pair of

une part de
a share/helping of

une tasse de
a cup of

une tranche de
a slice of

un verre de
a glass of

je voudrais une boîte de thon et un litre de lait
I'd like a tin of tuna and a litre of milk

il y a une boîte de limonade dans le frigo
there's a can of lemonade in the fridge

j'ai pris deux parts de frites
I took two helpings of chips

il a mangé une douzaine d'œufs et six morceaux de poulet
he ate a dozen eggs and six pieces of chicken

3 Expressions of quantity used without a noun

When an expression of quantity is not followed by a noun, de is replaced by the pronoun en (*see* pp 80-82):

> **il y avait beaucoup de neige; il y en avait beaucoup**
> there was a lot of snow; there was a lot (of it)

> **elle a mangé trop de chocolats; elle en a trop mangé**
> she's eaten too many chocolats; she's eaten too many (of them)

11 EXPRESSIONS OF TIME

A THE TIME

quelle heure est-il?
what time is it?

a) *full hours*

il est midi/minuit
it is 12 noon *or* midday/midnight

il est une heure
it is 1 o'clock

b) *half-hours*

il est minuit et demi(e)
it is 12.30 a.m./half past midnight

il est midi et demi(e)
it is 12.30 p.m.

il est une heure et demie
it is 1.30

c) *quarter-hours*

il est deux heures un/et quart
it is a quarter past two

il est deux heures moins le/un quart
it is a quarter to two

d) *minutes*

il est quatre heures vingt-trois
it is 23 minutes past four

il est cinq heures moins vingt
it is twenty to five

Note that minutes is usually omitted; heures is never omitted.

e) *a.m. and p.m.*

du matin
a.m., in the morning

de l'après-midi/du soir
p.m., in the evening

il est sept heures moins dix du matin
it is 6.50 a.m. *or* in the morning

il est sept heures dix du soir
it is 7.10 p.m *or* in the evening

The 24-hour clock is commonly used:

dix heures trente
10.30 a.m.

quatorze heures trente-cinq
2.35 p.m

dix-neuf heures dix
7.10 p.m.

Note that times are often abbreviated as follows:

dix-neuf heures dix
19h10

 B THE DATE

1 Names of months, days and seasons

a) *Months* (les mois)

janvier	January
février	February
mars	March
avril	April
mai	May
juin	June
juillet	July
août	August
septembre	September
octobre	October
novembre	November
décembre	December

b) *Days of the week* (les jours de la semaine)

lundi	Monday
mardi	Tuesday
mercredi	Wednesday
jeudi	Thursday
vendredi	Friday
samedi	Saturday
dimanche	Sunday

c) *Seasons* (les saisons)

le printemps	spring
l'été	summer
l'automne	autumn
l'hiver	winter

For prepositions used with the seasons see p 19.

Note that in French, months and days are masculine and do not have a capital letter unless they begin a sentence.

2 Dates

a) Cardinals (eg **deux, trois**) are used for the dates of the month except the first:

le quatorze juillet	**le deux novembre**
the fourteenth of July	the second of November
But: **le premier février**	
the first of February	

The definite article is used as in English; French does not use prepositions ('on' and 'of' in English):

je vous ai écrit le trois mars
I wrote to you on the third of March

b) **mil** (a thousand) is used instead of **mille** in dates from 1001 onwards:

mil neuf cent quatre-vingt sept
nineteen hundred and eighty-seven

l'an deux mil deux
the year two thousand and two

3 Année, journée, matinée, soirée

Année, journée, matinée and soirée (the feminine forms of an, jour, matin and soir) are usually found in the following cases:

a) *when duration is implied:*

pendant une année	for a (whole) year
toute la journée	all day long, the whole day
dans la matinée	in the (course of the) morning
passer une soirée	to spend an evening
l'année scolaire/universitaire	the school/academic year

b) *with an ordinal number or an indefinite expression:*

la deuxième année	the second year
dans sa vingtième année	in his twentieth year
plusieurs/quelques années	several/a few years
bien des/de nombreuses années	many years
environ une année	about a year

c) *with an adjective:*

de bonnes/mauvaises années	good/bad years

C IDIOMATIC EXPRESSIONS

à cinq heures	at five o'clock
à onze heures environ	(at) about eleven o'clock
vers minuit	(at) about midnight
vers (les) dix heures	(at) about ten o'clock
il est six heures passées	it's past six o'clock
à quatre heures précises/pile	at exactly four o'clock
sur le coup de trois heures	on the stroke of three
à partir de neuf heures	from nine o'clock onwards
peu avant sept heures	shortly before seven
peu après sept heures	shortly after seven

tôt ou tard	sooner or later
au plus tôt	at the earliest
au plus tard	at the latest
il est tard	it is late
il est en retard	he is late
il se lève tard	he gets up late
il est arrivé en retard	he arrived late
le train a vingt minutes de retard	the train is twenty minutes late
ma montre retarde de six minutes	my watch is six minutes slow
ma montre avance de six minutes	my watch is six minutes fast
ce soir	this evening, tonight
demain soir	tomorrow evening, tomorrow night
hier soir	yesterday evening, last night
samedi soir	Saturday evening
je sors samedi soir	I'm going out on Saturday night *or* evening
dans la soirée de samedi	on Saturday evening
dans la nuit de samedi (à dimanche)	during Saturday night
demain matin	tomorrow morning
hier matin	yesterday morning
lundi matin	Monday morning
j'y vais lundi matin	I'm going there on Monday morning
demain en huit	tomorrow week
le lendemain	the next day
le lendemain matin	the next morning
hier matin	yesterday morning
la semaine dernière	last week
la semaine prochaine	next week
la semaine qui vient	this coming week
je l'ai vu l'autre samedi	I saw him the other Saturday
lundi	on Monday
le lundi	on Mondays
je commence lundi	I'm starting (on) Monday
il vient le lundi	he comes on Mondays, he comes on a Monday
vient un lundi	come one Monday

un lundi sur deux	every other Monday, every second Monday
tous les lundis	every Monday
tous les lundis soirs	every Monday evening *or* night
tous mes lundis	all my Mondays
lundi en huit	a week on Monday, Monday week
lundi en quinze	a fortnight on Monday
il y a trois semaines	three weeks ago
il vient l'après-midi	he comes in the afternoon(s)
viens un après-midi	come one afternoon
une demi-heure	a half-hour, half an hour
un quart d'heure	a quarter of an hour
trois quarts d'heure	three quarters of an hour
passer son temps (à faire)	to spend one's time (doing)
perdre son temps	to waste one's time
de temps en temps	from time to time
de temps à autre	from time to time
dans les temps	on time
au début de l'après-midi/de la soirée, en début de l'après-midi/ de soirée	in the early afternoon/evening
je te téléphonerai au début de la matinée	I'll phone you first thing in the morning
au début du mois	at the beginning of the month
j'ai une réunion au milieu de la matinée *ou* en milieu de matinée	I have a meeting mid-morning
au milieu (du mois) de juin, (à la) mi-juin	in the middle of June, mid-June
au milieu de l'hiver	in the middle of winter, midwinter
j'ai une réunion à la fin de la matinée *ou* en fin de matinée	I have a meeting late morning
à la fin de l'hiver	at the end of the winter
on en reparlera fin janvier *ou* à la fin du mois de janvier	we'll talk about it again at the end of January
quel jour sommes-nous aujourd'hui?	what day is it today?

le combien sommes-nous aujourd'hui?	what's the date today?, what's today's date?
nous sommes/c'est le trois avril	it's the third of April
aujourd'hui nous sommes samedi	today is Saturday, it's Saturday today
vendredi 11 janvier 2002	Friday, 11 January 2002
nous nous sommes vus le vendredi 11 janvier	we saw each other on Friday, 11th January
le vendredi treize juillet	Friday the thirteenth of July
en février/au mois de février	in February/in the month of February
en février 2002	in February 2002
l'été 2002	in the summer of 2002, in summer 2002
en 2002	in 2002
dans les années soixante	in the sixties, in the 60s, in the 1960s
au début/à la fin des années soixante	in the early/late sixties
au dix-septième siècle	in the seventeenth century
au XVIIe	in the 17th century
le jour de l'An	New Year's Day
avoir treize ans	to be thirteen (years old)
être âgé de quatorze ans	to be fourteen (years old)
elle fête ses vingt ans	she's celebrating her twentieth birthday
elle a une vingtaine d'années	she's around twenty (years old)
un plan quinquennal	a five-year plan
une année bissextile	a leap year
une année civile	a calendar year
une année-lumière	a light year

12 THE SENTENCE

A WORD ORDER

Word order is usually the same in French as in English, except in the following cases:

1 Adjectives

Many French adjectives follow the noun (*see* pp 44-6):

de l'argent suédois
(some) *Swedish* money

j'ai les yeux bleus
I've got *blue* eyes

2 Adverbs

In simple tenses, adverbs usually follow the verb (*see* pp 56-7):

j'y vais rarement
I *seldom* go there

il fera bientôt nuit
it will *soon* be dark

3 Object pronouns

Object pronouns usually come before the verb (*see* pp 77-7):

je t'attendrai
I'll wait *for you*

il la lui a vendue
he sold *it* to him

4 Noun phrases

Noun phrases are formed differently in French (*see* pp 257-8):

une chemise en coton
a cotton shirt

le père de mon copain
my friend's father

5 Exclamations

The word order is not affected after que or comme (unlike after 'how' in English):

que tu es bête!
you *are* silly!/how silly you are!

qu'il fait froid!
it's so cold!

comme il chante mal!
he sings so badly!

comme c'est beau!
that's so beautiful!

6 Dont

Dont must be followed by the subject of the clause it introduces; compare:

l'ami dont j'ai perdu l'adresse
the friend whose address I lost

l'ami dont l'adresse a changé
the friend whose address has changed

7 Inversion

In certain cases, the subject of a French clause is placed after the verb. Word order is effectively that of an interrogative sentence (*see pp 243-5*). This occurs:

a) *after the following, when they occur at the beginning of a clause:*

à peine	aussi	peut-être
hardly	therefore	maybe, perhaps

à peine Alain était-il sorti qu'il a commencé à pleuvoir
Alain had barely gone out when it started raining

il y avait une grève du métro, aussi a-t-il pris un taxi
there was an underground strike, so he took a taxi

peut-être vont-ils téléphoner plus tard
maybe they'll phone later

> *But:*   **Alain était à peine sorti qu'il a commencé à pleuvoir**
> **ils vont peut-être téléphoner plus tard**

b) *when a verb of saying follows direct speech:*

'si tu veux', a répondu Marie
'if you want', Marie replied

'j'espère que non', dit-il
'I hope not', he said

'attention!' a-t-elle crié
'watch out!', she shouted

'répondez!' ordonna-t-il
'answer!', he ordered

B NEGATIVE EXPRESSIONS

1 Main negative words

a)

ne ... pas	not
ne ... point	not *(literary)*
ne ... plus	no more/ longer, not ... any more
ne ... jamais	never
ne ... rien	nothing, not ... anything
ne ... guère	hardly

b)

ne ... personne	nobody, no one, not ... anyone
ne ... que	only
ne ... ni (ni ... ni)	neither ... nor
ne ... aucun(e)	no, not any, none
ne ... nul(le)	no
ne ... nulle part	nowhere, not ... anywhere

Note

- ne becomes n' before a vowel or a silent h.

- aucun and nul, like other adjectives and pronouns, agree with the word they refer to; they are used only in the singular.

2 Position of negative expressions

a) *with simple tenses and with the imperative*

Negative words enclose the verb: ne comes before the verb, and the second part of the negative expression comes after the verb:

je ne la connais pas
I don't know her

je n'ai plus d'argent
I haven't any money left

ne dis rien
don't say anything

je n'avais que 3 euros
I only had 3 euros

tu n'as aucun sens de l'humour
you have no sense of humour

n'insistez pas!
don't insist!

tu ne le sauras jamais
you'll never know

il n'y a personne
no one's here

il n'est nulle part
it isn't anywhere

il n'est ni bête ni crédule
he's neither stupid nor gullible

b) *with compound tenses*

With ne ... pas and the other expressions in list 1 a, the word order is: ne + auxiliary + pas + past participle:

il n'est pas revenu
he didn't come back

je n'avais jamais vu Paris
I had never seen Paris

je n'ai plus essayé
I didn't try any more

on n'a rien fait
we haven't done anything

With ne ... personne and the other expressions in list 1 b, the word order is: ne + auxiliary + past participle + personne/que/ni *etc*:

il ne l'a dit à personne
he didn't tell anyone

je n'en ai aimé aucun
I didn't like any of them

tu n'en as acheté qu'un?
did you only buy one?

il n'est allé nulle part
he hasn't gone anywhere

c) *with the infinitive*

i) ne ... pas and the other expressions in list 1 a are placed together before the verb:

je préfère ne pas y aller
I'd rather not go

essaye de ne rien perdre
try not to lose anything

ii) ne ... personne and the other expressions in list **1 b** enclose the infinitive:

il a été surpris de ne voir personne
he was surprised not to see anybody

j'ai décidé de n'en acheter aucun
I decided not to buy any of them

d) *at the beginning of a sentence*

When personne, rien, aucun and ni ... ni ... begin a sentence, they are followed by ne:

personne ne le sait   **rien n'a changé**
nobody knows   nothing has changed

ni Paul ni Alain ne sont venus   **aucun secours n'est arrivé**
neither Paul nor Alain came   no help arrived

3 Combination of negative expressions

Negative expressions can be combined:

ne ... plus jamais	ne ... jamais rien
ne ... plus rien	ne ... jamais personne
ne ... plus personne	ne ... jamais ni ... ni
ne ... plus ni ... ni	ne ... jamais que
ne ... plus que	

on ne l'a plus jamais revu   **il n'y a plus rien**
we never saw him again   there isn't anything left

plus personne ne viendra   **tu ne dis jamais rien**
no one will come any more   you never say anything

je ne bois jamais que de l'eau   **je ne vois jamais personne**
I only ever drink water   I never see anybody

je ne pardonnerai jamais ni n'oublierai
I will never forgive nor forget

4 Negative expressions without a verb

a) pas

pas (not) is the most common of all negatives; it is frequently used without a verb:

tu l'aimes? – pas beaucoup
do you like it? – not much

ah non, pas lui!
oh no, not him!

non merci, pas pour moi
no thanks, not for me

un roman pas très long
not a very long novel

lui, il viendra, mais pas moi
he will come, but I won't

j'aime ça; pas toi?
I like that; don't you?

b) ne

ne is not used when there is no verb:

qui a crié? ... personne
who shouted? – nobody

jamais de la vie!
not on your life!

rien! je ne veux rien!
nothing! I want nothing!

rien du tout
nothing at all

c) non

non (no) is always used without a verb:

tu aimes la natation? – non, pas du tout
do you like swimming? – no, not at all

tu viens, oui ou non? – je crois que non
are you coming, yes or no? – I don't think so

Note that non plus means 'neither':

je ne le crois pas – moi non plus
I don't believe him – neither do I

je n'ai rien mangé – nous non plus
I haven't eaten anything – neither have we

C DIRECT AND INDIRECT QUESTIONS

1 Direct questions

There are three ways of forming direct questions in French:

a) *subject + verb* (+ *question word*)

The word order remains the same as in statements (subject + verb) but the intonation changes: the voice is raised at the end of the sentence. This is by far the most common question form in conversational French:

tu l'as acheté où?	**je peux téléphoner d'ici?**
where did you buy it?	can I phone from here?
vous prendrez quel train?	**tu me fais confiance?**
which train will you take?	do you trust me?
c'était comment?	**la gare est près d'ici?**
what was it like?	is the station near here?
le train part à quelle heure?	**cette robe me va?**
what time does the train leave?	does this dress suit me?

b) (*question word*) + est-ce que + *subject* + *verb*

This question form is also very common in conversation:

qu'est-ce que tu as?	**est-ce qu'il est là?**
what's the matter with you?	is he in?
est-ce que ton ami s'est amusé?	**où est-ce que vous avez mal?**
did your friend have a good time?	where does it hurt?

c) *inversion*

This question form is the most formal of the three, and the least commonly used in conversation:

i) If the subject is a pronoun, the word order is as follows:

(question word) + verb + hyphen + subject

où allez-vous?	**voulez-vous commander?**
where are you going?	do you wish to order?
quand est-il arrivé?	**avez-vous bien dormi?**
when did he arrive?	did you sleep well?

ii) If the subject is a noun, a pronoun referring to the noun is inserted after the verb, and linked to it with a hyphen:

(question word) + noun subject + verb + hyphen + pronoun

où ton père travaillait-il?	**Nicole en veut-elle?**
where did your father work?	does Nicole want any?

iii) -t- is inserted before il and elle when the verb ends in a vowel:

comment va-t-il voyager?	**aime-t-elle le café?**
how will he travel?	does she like coffee?
pourquoi a-t-il refusé?	**Marie viendra-t-elle?**
why did he refuse?	will Marie be coming?

Note that when a question word is used, modern French will often just invert the verb and the noun subject, without adding a pronoun; no hyphen is then necessary:

où travaille ton père?
where does your father work?

2 Indirect questions

a) *Definition*

Indirect questions follow a verb and are introduced by an interrogative word, eg:

ask him when he will arrive
I don't know why he did it

b) *Word order*

  i) The word order is usually the same as in statements: question word + subject + verb:

je ne sais pas s'il voudra
I don't know if he'll want to

dis-moi où tu l'as mis
tell me where you put it

il n'a pas dit quand il appellerait
he didn't say when he would phone

  ii) If the subject is a noun, the verb and subject are sometimes inverted:

demande-leur où est le camping
ask them where the campsite is

> *But:*   **je ne comprends pas comment l'accident s'est produit**
> I don't understand how the accident happened
> **il ne savait pas pourquoi elle avait l'air triste**
> he didn't know why she looked sad

3 Translation of English question tags

Question tags are phrases like: 'isn't it?', 'aren't you?', 'doesn't he?', 'won't they?', 'haven't you?', 'is it?', 'did you?' *etc.* Question tags are less common in French than in English. Some of them can, however, be translated in the following ways:

i) **N'est-ce pas?**

N'est-ce pas? is used at the end of a sentence when confirmation of a statement is expected:

c'était très intéressant, n'est-ce pas?
it was very interesting, wasn't it?

tu voudrais partir en vacances, n'est-ce pas?
you'd like to go on holiday, wouldn't you?

vous n'arriverez pas trop tard, n'est-ce pas?
you won't be arriving too late, will you?

ii) Hein? and non?

In conversation hein? and non? are often used after affirmative statements instead of n'est-ce pas:

il fait beau, hein?
the weather's nice, isn't it?

il est amusant, non?
he's funny, isn't he?

D ANSWERS ('YES' AND 'NO')

1 Oui, si and non

a) Oui and si mean 'yes' and are equivalent to longer affirmative answers such as 'yes, it is', 'yes, I will', 'yes, he has' *etc*:

tu m'écriras? – oui, bien sûr!
will you write to me? – (yes) of course I will

b) Non means 'no' and is equivalent to longer negative answers such as 'no, it isn't', 'no, I didn't' *etc*:

c'était bien? – non, on s'est ennuyé
was it good? – no, it wasn't, we were bored

2 Oui or si?

Oui and si both mean 'yes', but oui is used to answer an affirmative question, and si to contradict a negative question:

cette place est libre? – oui
is this seat free? – yes (it is)

tu n'aimes pas lire? – si, bien sûr!
don't you like reading? – yes, of course (I do)

13 TRANSLATION PROBLEMS

A GENERAL TRANSLATION PROBLEMS

1 French words not translated in English

Some French words are not translated in English, particularly:

a) *Articles*

Definite and indefinite articles are not always translated (*see* pp 17-22):

dans la société moderne	**les gens en ont assez!**
in modern society	people have had enough!

ah non! encore du riz! je déteste le riz!
oh no! rice again! I hate rice!

b) *Que*

Que meaning 'that' as a conjunction (*see* pp 220-21) or 'that'/'which'/'whom' as a relative pronoun (*see* pp 91-2) cannot be omitted in French:

j'espère que tu vas mieux	**elle pense que c'est vrai**
I hope you're better	she thinks it's true
celui que j'ai vu	**c'est un pays que j'aime**
the one I saw	it's a country I like

c) *Prepositions*

Some French verbs are followed by a preposition (+ indirect object) when their English equivalent takes a direct object without a preposition (*see* pp 200-03):

elle a téléphoné au médecin	**tu l'as dit à ton père?**
she phoned the doctor	did you tell your father?

d) Le

When le (it) is used in an impersonal sense (*see* **p 76**), it is not translated:

oui, je le sais	**dis-le-lui**
yes, I know	tell him

2 English words not translated in French

Some English words are not translated in French, for example:

a) *Prepositions*

i) with verbs which take an indirect object in English, but a direct object in French (*see* **p 200**):

tu l'as payé combien?	**écoutez cette chanson**
how much did you pay *for* it?	listen *to* this song

ii) in certain expressions (*see* **p 232**):

je viendrai te voir lundi soir
I'll come and see you *on* Monday night

b) *'Can'*

'Can' + verb of hearing or seeing (*see* **p 161**):

je ne vois rien!	**tu entends la musique?**
I can't see anything!	can you hear the music?

3 Other differences

a) *English phrasal verbs*

Phrasal verbs are verbs which, when followed by a preposition, take on a different meaning, eg 'to give up', 'to walk out'. They do not exist in French and are translated by simple verbs or by expressions:

to give up	to run away	to run across
abandonner	**s'enfuir**	**traverser en courant**

b) *English possessive adjectives*

English possessive adjectives (my, your *etc*) are translated by the French definite article (le/la/les) when parts of the body are mentioned (*see* p 88):

brush *your* teeth	he hurt *his* foot
brosse-toi les dents	**il s'est fait mal au pied**

c) *'From'*

'From' is translated by à with verbs referring to taking something away (*see* p 203):

he hid it *from* his parents	borrow some *from* your dad
il l'a caché à ses parents	**empruntes-en à ton père**

B SPECIFIC TRANSLATION PROBLEMS

1 Words ending in -ING

The English verbal form ending in **-ing** is translated in a number of ways in French:

a) *by the appropriate French tense (see p 122):*

he's speaking *(present tense)*	**il parle**
he was speaking *(imperfect)*	**il parlait**
he will be speaking *(future)*	**il parlera**
he has been speaking *(perfect)*	**il a parlé**
he had been speaking *(pluperfect)*	**il avait parlé**
he would be speaking *(conditional)*	**il parlerait**

b) *by a French present participle (see pp 151-2)*

   i) as an adjective:

un livre amusant	**c'est effrayant**
a funny book	it's frightening

ii) as a verb, with **en** (while/on/by doing something; *see* pp 152-3):

'ça ne fait rien', dit-il en souriant
'it doesn't matter', he said smiling

j'ai vu mes copains en sortant du lycée
I saw my friends when I was coming out of school

Note, however, that **en** + present participle cannot be used when the two verbs have different subjects, eg:

I saw my brother coming out of school
j'ai vu mon frère sortir du lycée/qui sortait du lycée

c) *by a present infinitive* (*see* pp 142-50):

i) after a preposition:

au lieu de rire   **avant de traverser**
instead of laughing   before crossing

ii) after verbs of perception:

je l'ai entendu appeler   **je l'ai vue entrer**
I heard him calling   I saw her going in

iii) after verbs of liking and disliking:

j'adore faire du camping   **tu aimes lire?**
I love camping   do you like reading?

iv) after verbs followed by **à** or **de**:

tu passes tout ton temps à ne rien faire
you spend all your time doing nothing

il a commencé à neiger   **continuez à travailler**
it started snowing   go on working

tu as envie de sortir?   **il doit finir de manger**
do you feel like going out?   he must finish eating

v) when an English verb ending in **-ing** is the subject of another verb:

attendre serait inutile   **écrire est une corvée!**
waiting would be pointless   writing is a real chore!

vi) when an English verb ending in **-ing** follows 'is' or 'was' *etc*:

mon passe-temps favori, c'est de lire
my favourite pastime is reading

d) *by a perfect infinitive (see p 151)*

   i) after **après** (after):

   j'ai pris une douche après avoir nettoyé ma chambre
   I had a shower after cleaning my room

   ii) after certain verbs:

regretter	**remercier de**	**se souvenir de**
to regret	to thank for	to remember

   j'ai regretté de leur en avoir parlé
   I regretted speaking to them about it

   il m'a remercié d'être allé le chercher
   he thanked me for going to pick him up

e) *by a noun*

   particularly when referring to sports, activities, hobbies *etc*:

le ski	**la natation**	**l'équitation**
skiing	swimming	horse-riding
la voile	**le patinage**	**le canoë**
sailing	skating	canoeing
la lecture	**la planche à voile**	**la cuisine**
reading	windsurfing	cooking
la boxe	**la lutte**	**la marche à pied**
boxing	wrestling	walking

2 It is (It's)

'It is' (it's) can be translated in three ways in French:

a) **il** *or* **elle** *(see p 75)*

   il or **elle** are used with the verb **être** to translate 'it is', 'it was'
   etc (+ adjective) when referring to a particular masculine or
   feminine noun (a thing, a place *etc*):

   merci de ta carte; elle était très amusante
   thanks for your card; it was very funny

   regarde ce blouson; il n'est vraiment pas cher
   look at this jacket; it really isn't that expensive

b) ce (*see* p 63)

ce (c' before a vowel) is used with the verb être to translate 'it is', 'it was' *etc* in two cases:

i) If être is followed by a word which is not an adjective on its own, ie by a noun, a pronoun, an expression of place *etc*:

c'était ta voix
it was your voice

c'est une grande maison
it's a big house

c'est moi! c'est Claude!
it's me! it's Claude!

c'est le tien?
is it yours?

c'est en France que tu vas?
is it France you're going to?

c'est pour lundi
it's for Monday

ii) If être is followed by an adjective which refers to something previously mentioned, such as an idea, an event or a fact, but not to a specific noun:

l'homme n'ira jamais sur Saturne; ce n'est pas possible
Man will never go to Saturn; it's not possible

j'ai passé mes vacances en Italie; c'était formidable!
I spent my holidays in Italy; it was great!

oh, je m'excuse! – ce n'est pas grave
oh, I'm sorry! – it's all right

c) il (*see* pp 118-21)

il is used to translate 'it is', 'it was' *etc* in three cases:

i) With être followed by an adjective + de or que, ie referring to something that follows, but not to a specific noun:

il est impossible de connaître l'avenir
it's impossible to know the future

il est évident que tu ne me crois pas
it's obvious you don't believe me

ii) To describe the weather (*see* p 118):

il y a du vent
it's windy

il faisait très froid
it was very cold

iii) With être to tell the time and in phrases relating to the time of day, or in such expressions as il **est temps de** (it's time to):

il est deux heures du matin   **il est tard!**
it's two in the morning   it's late!

il est temps de partir
it's time to go

Note that with other expressions of time, c'est is used:

c'est lundi ou mardi aujourd'hui?   **c'était l'été**
is it Monday or Tuesday today?   it was summer

3 To be

Although 'to be' is usually translated by être, it can also be translated in the following ways:

a) Avoir

i) avoir is used instead of être in many set expressions:

avoir faim/soif	to be hungry/thirsty
avoir chaud/froid	to be warm/cold
avoir peur/honte	to be afraid/ashamed
avoir tort/raison	to be wrong/right

ii) avoir is also used for age:

quel âge as tu?   **j'ai vingt-cinq ans**
how old are you?   I'm twenty-five

b) Aller

aller is used for describing health:

je vais mieux   **tout le monde va bien**
I am/feel better   everyone's fine

c) Faire

faire is used in many expressions to describe the weather
(*see* **p** 118):

il fait beau	**il fera chaud**
the weather's nice	it will be hot

Note that il y a can also be used to describe the weather, but only
before du/de la/des:

il y a du vent/des nuages/de la tempête
it's windy/cloudy/stormy

d) *Untranslated*

'To be' is not translated when it is the first part of an English
continuous tense; instead, the appropriate tense is used in
French (*see* **p** 122):

I'm having a bath	he was driving slowly
je prends un bain	**il conduisait lentement**

4 Any

'Any' can be translated in three different ways:

a) Du/de la/des *or* de (*see* **pp** 23-4)

The partitive article is used with a noun in negative and
interrogative sentences:

il ne mange jamais de viande	**tu veux du pain?**
he never eats meat	do you want any bread?

b) En (*see* **p** 81)

En is used to translate 'any' when it occurs without a noun in
negative and interrogative sentences:

je n'en ai pas	**il en reste?**
I haven't got any	is there any left?

c) N'importe quel(le)/quel(le)s or tout(e)/tou(te)s

These are used to translate 'any' (and 'every') when they mean 'no matter which':

il pourrait arriver à n'importe quel moment
he could arrive any time

prends n'importe quelle couleur, je les aime toutes
take any colour, I like them all

5 Anyone, anything, anywhere

Like 'any', these can be translated in different ways:

a) *in interrogative sentences:*

il y a quelqu'un?
is anyone in?

tu l'as vu quelque part?
did you see it anywhere?

il a dit quelque chose?
did he say anything?

b) *in negative sentences:*

il n'y a personne
there isn't anyone

je ne le vois nulle part
I can't see it anywhere

je n'ai rien fait
I didn't do anything

c) *in the sense of 'any' (and 'every'), 'no matter which':*

n'importe qui peut le faire
anyone can do that

il croit n'importe quoi
he believes anything

j'irai n'importe où
I'll go anywhere

n'importe quand
anytime

6 You, your, yours, yourself

French has two separate sets of words to translate 'you', 'your', 'yours', 'yourself':

a) Tu, te (t'), toi, ton/ta/tes, le tien *etc*

b) Vous, votre/vos, le vôtre *etc*

For their respective meanings and uses, see pp 74-5, 84-5, 86-8, 89-90.

a) Tu *etc*

Tu, te, ton *etc* correspond to the tu form of the verb (second person singular) and are used when speaking to one person you know well (a friend, a relative) or to someone younger. They represent the familiar form of address:

si tu viens au concert avec ton copain, je t'achète deux places; une pour toi et une pour lui
if *you*'re coming to the concert with *your* boyfriend, I'll get *you* two tickets; one for *you* and one for him

b) Vous *etc*

Vous, vos *etc* correspond to the vous form of the verb (second person plural) and are used:

   i) when speaking to more than one person:

   dépêchez-vous, les gars! Vous allez manquer le train
   hurry up, guys! *You*'ll miss the train

   ii) when speaking to one person you do not know well or to someone older. They represent the formal or polite form of address:

   je regrette, Monsieur, mais vous ne pouvez pas garder votre chien avec vous dans ce restaurant
   I'm sorry, sir, but *you* can't keep *your* dog with *you* in this restaurant

c) When speaking or writing to one person, you must not mix words from both sets, but decide whether you are being formal or familiar, and use the same form of address throughout:

Cher Michel,
   Merci de ta lettre. Comment vas-tu? ...
Dear Michel,
   Thanks for *your* letter. How are *you*? ...

Monsieur,
   Pourriez-vous me réserver une chambre dans votre hôtel pour le 8 juin?
Dear Sir,
   Could *you* book a room for me in *your* hotel for 8th June?

Vous *etc* and **tu** *etc* can only be used together when **vous** is plural (ie when it refers to more than one person):

tu **sais, Jean, toi et ta sœur, vous vous ressemblez**
you know, Jean, *you* and *your* sister look like *each other*

7 Noun phrases

A noun phrase is a combination of two nouns used together to name things or people. In English, the first of these nouns is used to describe the second one, eg 'a love story'. In French, however, the position of the two nouns is reversed, so that the describing noun comes second and is linked to the first one by the preposition de (or d'):

une histoire d'amour a love story	**une feuille d'impôts** a tax form
un magasin de sport a sports shop	**un acteur de cinéma** a film actor
un arrêt d'autobus a bus stop	**un film d'aventure** an adventure film
un coup de soleil sunstroke	**une boule de neige** a snowball

un roman de science-fiction
a science-fiction novel

un match de football
a football match

le château d'Édimbourg
Edinburgh castle

un conte de fées
a fairy tale

un joueur de rugby
a rugby player

un employé de bureau
an office worker

Note that when the describing noun refers to a type of material, the preposition en is often used instead of de:

un pull en laine
a woollen jumper

un pantalon en cuir
leather trousers

une bague en or
a gold ring

un sac en plastique
a plastic bag

8 Possession

In English, possession is often expressed by using a noun phrase and tagging **'s** at the end of the first word, eg:

my friend's cat

This is translated in French by: object + de + possessor:

le chat de mon ami

Note the use of the article le/la/les.

le fiancé de ma sœur
my sister's fiancé

les amis de Claire
Claire's friends

les événements de la semaine dernière
last week's events

When **'s** is used to refer to someone's house or shop *etc*, it is translated by the preposition chez:

je téléphone de chez Paul
I'm phoning from Paul's (house)

chez le dentiste
at/to the dentist's

INDEX